THE Thousand-Mile Summer

Also by Colin Fletcher

The Complete Walker III
The Man from the Cave
The New Complete Walker
The Winds of Mara
The Man Who Walked Through Time
The Complete Walker

THE Thousand-Mile Summer

Colin Fletcher

VINTAGE BOOKS
A Division of Random House
New York

First Vintage Books Edition, April 1987

 Published in the United States by Random House, Inc., New York, and simultaneously in Canada by Random House of Canada Limited, Toronto. Originally published by Howell-North Books in hardcover in 1964 and in softcover in 1982.

Library of Congress Cataloging in Publication Data
Fletcher, Colin.
The thousand-mile summer.
Reprint. Original published: Berkeley, Calif.: Howell-North Books, 1964.
1. California—Description and travel—1951–1980. 2. Fletcher, Colin—Journeys—California. 3. Walking—California. I. Title.
F866.2.F55 1987 917.94 86-40464
ISBN 0-394-74631-7

Manufactured in the United States of America
10 9 8 7 6 5 4 3 2 1

Map by David Lindroth

To
Tim

It is better for the emissaries returning from the wilderness to record their marvel, not to define its meaning.

—Loren Eiseley

Contents

Preface

Time has given this book a dimension I did not plan.

During my thousand-mile summer I sometimes became aware that I was watching a passing show. But as I walked through those free and sumptuous days, rich with the rewards of inexperience, I did not know that man would soon lay a heavy, engineering hand on much of the land I was seeing. It has happened, though. And now, almost a quarter of a century later, those who know today's California—today's America, today's world—may perhaps find in the book a quiet testimony not only to the past but also, I hope, to the road we must walk in the future.

C.F.
California
Winter 1981

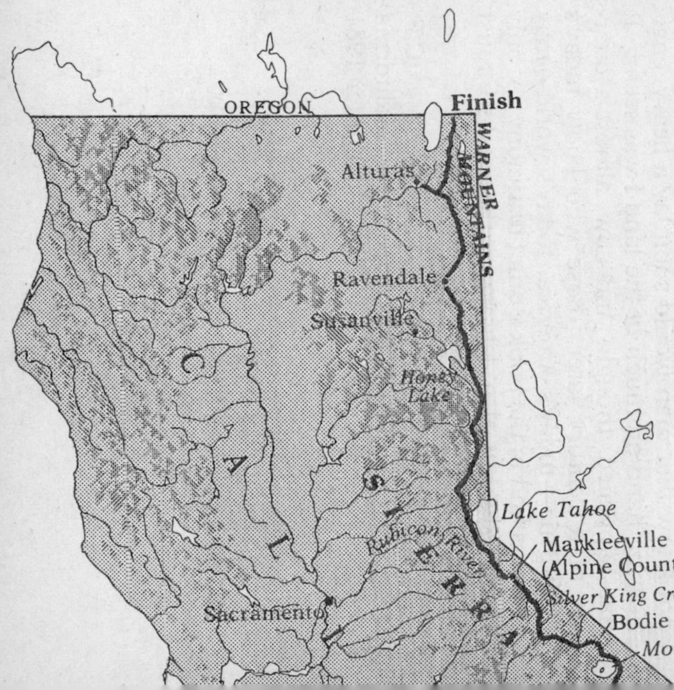

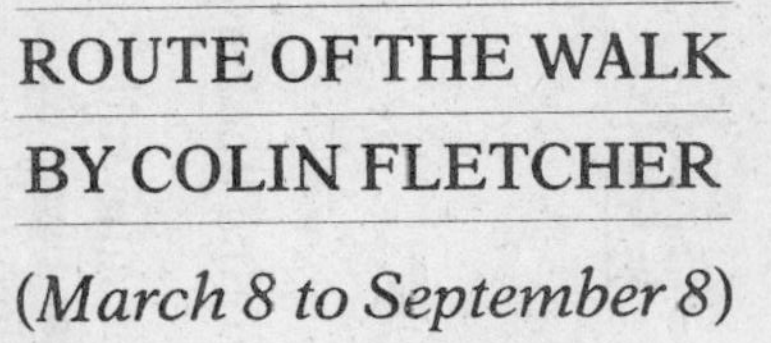

ROUTE OF THE WALK

BY COLIN FLETCHER

(March 8 to September 8)

NEVADA
EUREKA VALLEY
DEATH VALLEY
Fresno
Bakersfield
PACIFIC OCEAN
MOJAVE DESERT
Baker
Goffs
Needles
ARIZONA
Earp
Parker Dam
Colorado River
Los Angeles
Blythe
Palo Verde
Picacho
Yuma
Start
San Diego
MEXICO
0
100 Miles
0
100 Kilometers

THE Thousand-Mile Summer

CHAPTER 1

IN SAN FRANCISCO

Ideas that burst on you at three o'clock in the morning, looking as if they will change your life, have a despicable habit of losing their luster in daylight. But very occasionally—once or twice in a lifetime—they fulfill their promise, right to the end.

I was lying awake in my San Francisco apartment one February night, worrying about the things we all worry about, when it came to me out of nowhere, without the apparent aid of logic, that what I wanted most in life just then was to walk from one end of California to the other. I lay still, no longer tossing and turning. I knew, of course, that the idea was crazy; but I felt almost sure I was going.

Next morning the idea still glittered. A week later it still had me half dazzled. And by then I was quite sure.

At first I did not worry about reasons: my mountain of personal problems had shrunk to a molehill, and that was enough. But when, inevitably, people asked why I was going, I found I had no sort of answer ready. After a while, I began to say that I wanted to "take a look at America."

It was true enough too, as far as it went. Ever

since moving to the United States two years earlier I had been hankering for a broader look; and I could hardly have hit on a more varied sample than I would find in a six-month, one-thousand-mile walk—off the road wherever possible—from Mexico to Oregon. But mainly, of course, I gave the answer in self-defense. It isn't easy to explain to a stranger (or to anyone else for that matter) a network of half-understood desires for change, open spaces, simplicity, physical challenge, money, and the opportunity to stand aside from the turmoil and see where you are going. None of these reasons quite satisfied me anyway. So I adopted, as a convenient peg on which to hang something even more worthwhile, the rather brittle statement that I was going out to "discover America."

There was, in any case, precious little time for worrying about reasons. I had made up my mind to travel through California's unspoiled and relatively little-known eastern regions—desert in the south, mountain range in the north. I soon decided that, in order to reach the mountains after the worst snow had melted, I would go from south to north. And that meant I had to start within a month; otherwise I would find the desert—Death Valley in particular—stoked up into a furnace.

It turned out to be a hectic month. Soon, my apartment furniture disappeared under an avalanche of maps, and I found myself eat-and-sleep deep in routes and loads, clothing and cameras, sleeping bags and pemmican. I grudged every hour at my stopgap job as hospital janitor, every minute away from The Walk's logistic problems.

My backpacking experience was meager: a few short trips during five years of farming in Kenya;

two summers of semi-civilized prospecting in British Columbia. But back in Britain during World War II, I had grappled at close and sweaty quarters with the problem of what a man can and cannot carry, and I knew that if you look after the ounces the pounds look after themselves. So during that hectic month I went shopping with a postal scale and checked like gold dust every item from salt tablets to jockey shorts.

The final week was taut with detail: last-minute equipment decisions, arrangements for processing and storage of film, solution of money problems, conferences with the *San Francisco Chronicle* about an article series, and mailing ahead maps and dehydrated food to the remote post offices I would call in at every couple of weeks. At times I despaired of meeting the deadline.

But at last, after a hurried detour through Death Valley to cache out three 5-gallon cans of drinking water, I found myself beside the Colorado River at the Mexican border, waving good-bye to the friend who was driving my old station wagon back to San Francisco. And there at the border, at a back-road customs post, I found that I had already begun to "discover America."

On the Mexican side of the customs gate, a phonograph blared music down a dusty, sun-drenched street. A man who might have been planted there by a travel agent slept on a broken adobe wall—head and shoulders eclipsed by a huge sombrero, body fitting the jagged wall like a model's in one of those fatuous mattress advertisements.

California had gone Spanish too. The U.S. customs officer lolled on his patio in a wicker chair, and at his feet squatted a Mexican boy. The boy was a craftsman. He buffed and polished and burnished the customs officer's elegant knee boots until their radiance threatened to set the dry scrub on fire. The boy sat back at last, and the customs officer inspected his boots. He rotated them slowly, first one, then the other, like a mannequin. Finally he nodded approval and tossed down a coin. "The kid's a good polisher," he said, and you knew his day was made.

The customs officer stood up, stepped to the edge of his patio, and shook hands with me. Somehow, he managed to make that a solemn little ceremony too. "And the best of luck, all the way," he said.

I swung the fifty-pound pack onto my back, walked to the customs gate, and put one foot in Mexico. Then I turned and took my first step northward along the dusty road.

I walked slowly, struggling to break out of a sudden, aching vacuum—the vacuum that so often clamps down when you sever your last ties with the familiar and face the unknown. I knew, of course, that the depression would pass. And I knew as well that all I had really begun was my shakedown cruise. Upriver for thirty miles, irrigation had tamed the desert; across that fertile strip of farmland I could walk at leisure and in safety. But beyond Imperial Dam stretched virgin desert. That was where the challenge would begin.

CHAPTER

2

UP THE COLORADO

I stood beside Imperial Dam, on the edge of an immense silence. As far north as I could see stretched a jumble of parched brown peaks. Their eroded foothills reached down toward the Colorado like groping tentacles. The broad river was soon lost among them.

I stood for a while looking at the mountains and listening to the silence. Then I walked slowly out into the desert that for six hundred miles would be my world.

It was a strange and unexpected world. Like most people, I had let my mind accept the conventional image of the desert: a barren wasteland—hostile, cruel, and inhuman; flat sand stretching supine beneath a pitiless sun; mile after mile of monotony, broken only by cacti and occasional skulls.

The world I found above Imperial Dam was none of these things. The jagged peaks did not threaten; they held aloof. The groping foothills rolled stark and arid, but now that I was among them I felt no cruelty. And once I had escaped the works of man there was no more inhumanity.

Mile after mile, my feet crunched on stones or padded over solid rock; they were silent only in washes, or valleys, where the sand stretched soft and level as on vacation beaches. And the sun beamed down from a Mediterranean sky, with friendly white clouds drifting by like "Welcome" banners. A breeze caressed my bare arms and legs.

At every turn I met not monotony but vivid contrast. A chocolate rock face sliced off to startling red. The crest of a ridge, planed flat as if by a giant carpenter, dropped sheer into a sandy wash. The wash was rich with bushes and flowers, and a few indomitable trees clung to life with knotted roots. Beyond, a pale green plateau humped and buckled into minor peaks, some bare and round as buttocks, some pointed and tipped with brown, like conical coconut cakes that had been slightly overdone.

And always the desert was alive. A sandpiper questioned me from a rock, took flight without its answer, and slanted away across the river. A slumbering lizard opened one piercing eye—and was gone. And for a week I walked among caterpillars. The little black furry creatures were everywhere, wriggling furiously to nowhere. They bustled in their hundreds of thousands over rock and sand and up onto the bushes and flowers.

The flowers dominated everything, turning the desert into a garden. Sunflowers, swiveling with the sun, painted whole washes yellow. I climbed a ridge and its "bare" brown slopes became a waving field of white and purple. Close against the stones pressed little daisies and violets that I did not see until my feet were almost on them. And if I knelt down I discovered an even fainter carpet, each flower so delicate that it made the violets look cumbersome. I was glad I was no botanist. I might be missing rare specimens; but if I had been grubbing about among names and technicalities I might have missed the wonder of that prodigal and endless display. For the flowers went on and on. I wondered how far back they stretched into the brown and arid mountains to the west.

To the east rose more mountains. But they were beyond the barrier of the Colorado, in Arizona, and they might as well have been on a different planet. Their distant ridges, groping down toward the river too, looked like a parched wasteland, incapable of supporting flowers. Only the thin logical layer of my mind accepted that they were a replica of the clean and cheerful desert I was walking through.

It is hard to say why virgin desert looks so clean. Partly, I suppose, because the sun has purged it. Partly because your eye seems to pierce to the heart of everything. A creosote bush is too skimpy to hold secrets. Every wrinkle of a distant escarpment stands out so clear and close that you want to run your hand over it and feel the roughness. Only man defiles. For the frankness that makes the desert so pure also leaves it wide open to rape. Wheel tracks last for years, bulldozer scars for decades. A derelict house looks as if it will stand stark and hideous until Judgment Day.

Back near the Mexican border, away from irrigation, I had crossed a few isolated waste patches that were desert of sorts. But they had been on the defensive, almost in hiding. Here above Imperial Dam the desert ruled. My mind is of the kind eager to detect human attributes in nature (a habit that makes pedants shuffle away muttering "Anthropomorphism!" or "Pathetic fallacy!") and I saw this new and regal desert as an autocrat. A benevolent and peace-loving autocrat, omnipotent and sure of itself, gentle in the assurance of its power. As long as a man understood and obeyed its laws, he had nothing to fear.

I felt content that this was the desert that for six hundred miles would be my world.

For the first two hundred miles, my lifeline through it would be the Colorado. I had expected the river to be a companion as well. But from the first it held aloof. Its main channel flowed broad and strong; but the channel was not the whole river. On either side spread beds of tules—or bulrushes. Mile after mile they stretched, thick and green. Among them glinted open lakes. And lagoons pushed far back into the desert. On my large-scale map the river was a blue snake twisting among the tatters of its discarded blue skin.

When I climbed to the crest of a ridge I sometimes saw the main river, but it was usually a mile or more away. Even at night camps, when I had to have water, I could rarely get closer than the tip of an outlying lagoon.

Then, one morning when an unusual gray overcast blanketed the sky, I stopped to rest at the point of a ridge. For the first time, I found the main channel racing past almost at my feet. Upstream, it stretched leaden and somber, seeming to pour out of distant black clouds. Downstream, it swept around a bend and vanished among barren hills.

And there on the ridge I heard for the first time the voice of the Colorado. It was a deep and powerful voice. It had none of the music of a mountain stream, none of the caress of a meandering river. Swirls and eddies muttered dark threats, as if striving to impress the desert. Its waters might be harnessed by dams, it seemed to say, but it had not surrendered to man—and it never would. Hearing the river's voice, I understood for the first time warnings that I should not trust the Colorado, that it was "an unfriendly river," that it "didn't like people." Lifeline or no, I saw, the river would always threaten.

At Imperial Dam, a fisherman had told me what to expect in the sixty or seventy miles before I reached the first real settlement, at Palo Verde. "Along that stretch of river," he said, "you'll find about the last corner of California that you can still call the old frontier. Why, there's an old man living in an adobe hut near Picacho who says he knew Wyatt Earp."

For a week I traveled along this old frontier.

At first I passed through the virgin America that early settlers found. Then I began to stumble on relics the frontiersmen had left behind, like old props on a deserted stage.

The play had told the story of an early skirmish in man's long struggle with the Colorado.

Ever since the white man came West he has been striving to tame the Colorado. And the river has been fighting back. The weapons in the struggle have been erosion and irrigation ditches, floods and levees, droughts and dams and power stations. And the story of the campaign is written on the desert. For the river and the desert it runs through are inextricably linked. The river's color, and so its name, derives from red desert soil. And the desert bears the river's imprint. Loops of discarded riverbed create sloughs or depressions or deep canyons. And the ridges and washes have been eroded into existence by water draining down from the mountains into the trough the river has dug for itself.

So when man tames the river he tames the desert

too. Below Imperial Dam he has channeled the water through a network of irrigation ditches and transformed a flat desert plain into fertile farmland. Above the dam, the river has kept its freedom; but man long ago pushed out patrols, met fierce resistance, and was forced to withdraw. Here and there he made his little marks on the desert's surface. And the desert preserved the marks as relics, as discarded stage props of American history.

I had studied the stage directions in advance. The maps read like the script of a western soap opera: Bear Gulch Bluff, Regan Slough, Adobe Lake, Draper Ranch, 4S Ranch. But Draper and 4S ranches turned out to be pathetic little huddles of warped and weathered buildings, mere empty shells, twenty miles apart.

The ranches were set in a dried-out version of the rangeland every TV viewer knows like his own backyard. Canyons wound deep and dusty. Bluffs soared up foursquare against the sky. And through this rough country I at first made slow progress. Once it took me six hours to go three straight-line miles.

But I made better time once I had passed what the map called "Picacho (Ruins)." Somehow I missed this mining relic of the old frontier. All I saw was a dirt road running in from the outside world and a few more or less modern shacks among the dusty scrub. But beyond Picacho I hit the Wetback Trail.

The Trail ran north, parallel to the river. It was at once a part and yet not a part of the old frontier. Like a wall that persists through several layers of an archaeological excavation, it had been there before the ranches, continued through their life span, and long outlasted them.

Mexicans first made the Wetback Trail almost a century ago. And they have been using it off and on ever since. People had told me that not long before they were pouring through every day, groups of twenty or thirty at a time. But now the U.S. Border Patrol kept a strict watch, and not many wetbacks braved the eighty-mile gauntlet of man and nature between the border and Palo Verde. Even fewer succeeded.

The wetbacks had a fine eye for country. Traveling without maps through wildly confusing terrain, they almost always chose the best route. I felt very humble—until I remembered that different men have different limitations. Give a wetback a map and he will use it to light a fire. Turn him loose on Main at First and he will be helpless as a sailor in the desert.

Only once did I attempt to second-guess the trailmakers. The detour showed me how superficially man ever "tamed" the desert. And I learned something of the resistance the frontiersmen had met—and why they had been forced to withdraw. I learned the answer to another question too.

One morning I stopped to rest on a high mesa. Ahead, bare brown ridges stretched across my path as far as I could see. They were long and steep and confused, and I knew the Trail would wind up and down and around them, mile after mile, hour after hour. I checked the map. It showed a narrow canyon swinging up and away from the river behind the first line of mountain peaks; from its head another canyon cut back to the river several miles ahead. A detour through the canyons might save half a day of up-and-down slogging.

The detour had its possible drawbacks though. I

had heard of wetback skeletons being found in remote canyons, years after their owners had lost the way. Two U.S. Border Patrolmen who tracked me down as a suspect wetback the afternoon I left the border had said that if I failed to reach Palo Verde on schedule they would organize a search. I knew, though, that if anything went wrong while I was detouring through the side canyons, nobody would stand much chance of finding me.

But ever since I first saw those parched mountains I had been waiting for the chance to explore them.

At the next lagoon I filled one of my two half-gallon canteens, dropped in a couple of water-purifying tablets, and headed west, away from my lifeline.

The canyon began as an insignificant cleft that slid out, backhand, between two rock ridges. It was heavily camouflaged with mesquite trees. Nobody without a map could have guessed where it led.

Beyond the entrance, a strip of sand snaked away between steep walls. The last flash flood to sweep down from the mountains had left piles of dead twigs and branches and whole tree trunks to the summer sun. There was no breeze, and the sun glared back from pale sand.

Soon I was hurrying up rock and rubble slopes. Bright flowers softened the brick-red harshness. The slopes steepened. But I came to no serious obstacles, and two hours after leaving the Wetback Trail I climbed up out of the canyon head onto an open plateau. And there I found the answer to one of my first desert questions.

All around me, bare brown rock stretched toward a horizon of blunt peaks and stiletto pinnacles. In all that immense sweep of brown rock and brown stones I could see no sign of life. Nowhere except at my feet. There, flowers pushed up between the stones and through cracks in the rock. But their yellows and whites and purples spread only a few yards. Beyond, the brownness began. I slipped off my pack and walked forward to a squat beavertail cactus that blazed out with a splash of vivid magenta. To my surprise, flowers grew thick around it. I walked forward again to an ocotillo plant that reached up with red-tipped tentacles like a sun-worshiping octopus. Then I looked down—and found my feet still surrounded by flowers. I looked back at my pack. It stood on bare brown rock. And all at once I understood that the barren mountains were not really barren. I knew—though I found it difficult to believe—that in whichever direction I walked over the brown rock, toward whichever peak along that jagged horizon, the flowers would come with me.

After a while I started down the second canyon. This, I knew, was the real test. It is always harder to climb down than up.

The canyon began as a steep gully. Soon it bit deep. Fierce buttresses thrust out from its walls. Massive overhangs held shadows from the sun. In their coolness the furry black caterpillars swarmed thick and seething. Once, the canyon spilled down a fault so narrow that to squeeze through I had to take off my pack and pull it after me. Once, I had to tie the pack to a nylon cord and lower it down a rock face. I dropped my yucca walking staff down too, then climbed after it and found a natural basin that still held water from the last rains. The water was green and fetid and coated with the black caterpillars; but any water was a comforting sight.

The canyon cut deeper. On either side, eroded rock pinnacles succeeded each other endlessly, like prison bars. I trudged on over soft sand. My feet sank into it. Each time I eased the pack on my back, a new runnel of sweat trickled down and joined the swamp around my waist. Complicated ideas no longer penetrated my mind; the sun had browned it with an opaque crust. Lunchtime was long overdue; but I had made up my mind to get back in sight of the river before I stopped to eat, and now it needed too much effort to alter the decision. I was conscious only of heat and dryness and glare and hunger.

I plodded on down the winding, walled-in strip of sand. The heat beat down, heavier and heavier. Then, quite suddenly, the walls fell back and I was standing in a broad wash and a breeze was blowing down from the mountains. Ten minutes later I saw the cool glint of the Colorado.

When I hit the Wetback Trail again, I realized it was the first sign of man since I struck away from the river, four hours earlier.

Although the desert had forced the frontiersmen to withdraw, their cattle seemed to have stayed on. I kept meeting trios and quartets of Hereford steers and heifers browsing in the washes. They would stare at me for a moment in disbelief, then career away like steeplechasers. They were plump and sleek, and I kept wondering who they belonged to.

The cattle had in places scuffed the Wetback Trail into a shallow trench. But more often it was just a faint, foot-wide track across the ridges, worn clear of plants and large flowers. There, it was easy to follow. But in the washes, with their sandy surfaces erased almost every year by flash floods, it petered out. The washes often measured a mile across, and it was some time before I learned to sense where the Trail would start again on the far side.

Every few miles I came across a smashed gallon-size wine bottle lying beside the Trail. There was only one other sign of the thousands of men who must have passed that way. One morning, miles from anywhere, I came to two flat-roofed bough-and-adobe huts beside the river. Among the many names scrawled on the inside walls, only one was non-Latin.

In the fifteen miles before the first outposts of Palo Verde Valley, I saw only one more stage prop from the old frontier.

The Trail swung out to the tip of a ridge and skirted the burnt-out site of a house. Uncut stones, barely a foot high, traced the outline of a single small room. Outside stood a massive iron cooking stove, cracked and rusty. The house overlooked a tule-ringed lake and commanded a view of the river, upstream and down, for many miles. The view was blue and green and pink and brown.

It was almost time for the hourly halt, so I slipped off my pack and sat down in the flowers beside the stove.

Below me, a light wind sandpapered the lake. Tules whispered together. In the distance, the river moved majestically past. Beyond, the desert rolled endlessly away: wash succeeded ridge; ridge succeeded wash. The world held nothing but openness and color, stillness and subtle movement, silence and gentle murmur.

I found myself dreaming of an old man living out his last years in this simple stone house—alone, untroubled and content. It would be difficult to find a better place for a man at peace with himself. I imagined this old frontiersman ferrying his new, unassembled stove downriver and carrying it, piece by piece, up to the house he had built. I imagined him sitting each evening in the shade of its stone walls and smiling to himself as he looked up and down the river that was "his." I imagined him . . .

I sat up with a jerk. The halt had already run to double its allotted ten minutes. I heaved the pack onto my back and hurried on northward along the Wetback Trail.

Far too often still, I found myself hurrying ahead like this. All through the hectic month of preparation I had thought that once I was on my way I would throw off the city's urgency. But now The Walk seemed in danger of becoming a race against time.

I was still fighting one real deadline. To avoid the risk of unbearable heat, I had to be through Death Valley by May 1. That meant reaching the south end of the Valley no later than mid-April. Three hundred and fifty miles—and almost six weeks to do it in. In theory, that was less than ten miles a day. It sounded easy enough. But the going would often be rough, and I had no intention of rushing past everything of interest. I was in no physical shape for pushing hard either: I had started with soft feet, a layer of city fat, and a fifty-pound pack that felt as though it weighed a ton and a half. So the pressure was there from the start.

I had known these things all along, of course. But there turned out to be one time-consuming factor I had not taken into account.

Back in San Francisco, a friend had said, "You'll be doing something we most of us need to do occasionally—bringing yourself back to earth by grappling with concrete problems instead of our eternal abstract ones."

Now, the concrete problems ruled my life. The four-day shakedown cruise had helped; but it had not shaken everything down. I still seemed to spend hours on the food problem—experimenting with menus, doling out dehydrated crumbs like a miser, or calculating whether the reserves would last to Palo Verde. Then there was cooking. Dead brush for firewood lay everywhere, and its sparks created no danger (the desert is curiously immune to arson); but kitchen technique with new equipment and strange food was an affair of time-consuming trial and error. And when I was not walking or cooking I seemed to be adjusting pack-load or shoulder straps, washing socks, washing feet, rubbing them with alcohol to harden the skin, or sprinkling them with powder. (A deep blister at this stage could be worse than a worn tire at the start of a transcontinental car rally.) More time went in studying maps and cutting margins off them to save weight. The weight problem was always there. I found myself conducting tense debates on whether to discard my fork, then making a phrenetic decision to pare down another fraction of an ounce by tearing off all tea-bag labels. And all the time my mind turned a treadmill of worries: water, route, campsite, photography, rattlesnakes, and a thousand inconsiderable trifles.

Such preoccupations may sound ridiculous; but anyone who has traveled alone on foot will recognize them. In your tight little world the smallest problem is liable to blow up without warning and fill the horizon. One day, high on a ridge, I stopped to change film. The circular fixture on the base of the camera case refused to turn. Without pliers I was helpless. The sun lost its brightness. The next fifty miles were suddenly populated with a torrent of torturingly photogenic subjects. I should never come this way again, and the chance of a lifetime would be lost forever. After an eternity that ticked on for three minutes I remembered the nylon cord in my pack. I wrapped it around the camera fixture and pulled. The fixture turned. The sun regained its brightness.

In my pack were a five-piece fishing rod and a paperback book, the first of a five-volume philosophy series I planned to finish before Oregon. By the end of a week I had fished for a grand total of half an hour and had read less than two pages. The book was useful though: it slid into the front of the pack and stopped pointed articles gouging my back. That was a concrete problem—one of the concrete problems that still seemed to rule almost every hour of the day. In other words, my shakedown cruise was not really over yet.

But I must not overstress this preoccupation with trivia. You cannot walk alone through virgin desert, day after day, without responding to the solitude. You do not grow lonely; you pass over instead into an aloneness that leaves you free and content.

The fifth evening beyond Imperial Dam I camped beside a lagoon. I was washing at a gap in its fringe of tules when the sun set behind a line of hills. The sudden coolness made me lift my head. Shadow already covered the lagoon and was climbing up the tules beyond. Above them, far beyond the hidden river, the Arizona mountains shone like molten gold. The shadow climbed higher and snuffed the last light from the tules. A bird cried once, and then was silent.

I stood still, waiting for the light to go out over the mountains too.

But the mountains were not yet ready. A line of golden peaks caught fire. Black canyons gouged their slopes and pierced the iridescent red with deeper hints of hell. The iridescence deepened, the hints broadened. And then—on the very threshold of revelation—the shadow reached out and quieted everything, and the world was only shades of gray.

I found myself shivering on the edge of the lagoon, still clutching a cake of soap.

After supper I sat in front of my fire, torpid and happy. The tules were busy now with rustles and swirls and mysterious sucking noises. Frogs gargled the night air. The firelight flickered creosote bushes into existence one moment and banished them the next. In the distance, coyotes yowled. When the air grew cold and I slid into my mummy bag, I left some slack in the securing tapes and hollowed an opening above one ear. Only my nose and eyes and mouth were free, but I could still hear nightlife among the tules. All I could see until I fell asleep was the blackness of the desert sky, with the stars sometimes pasted on its surface and sometimes receding for ever and ever.

I opened my eyes. The blue sky was filled with huge white birds, tinged pink by the rising sun. They soared and circled in solid phalanx, lifting and eddying with the wind, gliding on immense black-tipped wings. Faintly, I heard the music of air rushing through feathers.

In that huge formation there was nearly always

at least one bird beating its wings to hold position. But from time to time came a moment when every wing was stilled and the phalanx swept across the sky in majestic unity. Each interval of stillness and soaring movement was so simple and beautiful that I found my muscles tensing as I tried to grasp the moment and force it to endure. Then another pair of wings would beat and I could relax.

The flight began to break up. The sky to the north filled with scattered groups, all soaring, wheeling, and seeking. They moved farther and farther away until finally, even when I scrambled from my sleeping bag and ran up onto a ridge, I could no longer see them.

That morning I walked exultantly, still remembering the poetry of flight. But I walked reluctantly as well. I did not want to leave this unspoiled country where the flowers went on and on and where huge birds soared in peace. I wanted to linger and explore this refuge where the Colorado had held man at bay, this ghost of the old frontier where only the frontiersmen were missing—or so it seemed. But I kept remembering my Death Valley deadline. And I had less than a day's food left, and it was still twenty-five miles to Palo Verde. The map showed several isolated buildings about fifteen miles south of Palo Verde. They might or might not be occupied.

By the time I reached the first building it was past noon, and the Wetback Trail had merged with a jeep road. The cabin stood close to the river, on a low gravel spit. I climbed up onto the spit.

An acre of desert had been bulldozed into the twentieth century. Within that acre there were no flowers, no bushes, no rocks, no little gullies, no unevenness with any meaning. In the center squatted the cabin. Black shingles sheathed roof and walls. Alongside, an ancient truck had settled on flattened tires. The bare gravel was littered with old oil drums, a rusty wheelbarrow, and several mattresses. A garbage heap was crowned by a broken doll. A sign upended against a cement mixer read: FISHING AND HUNTING IN COLORADO RIVER.

I sat down under a lean-to roof and brewed tea and my last package of soup. I tried to forget the open gravel, but the glare was too insistent. And a shadow on my left kept resolving into the hood of the truck. From a winch on its bumper a cable wound limply away and out of sight.

A faint sound made me look up. A small dust devil was advancing across the desert. It reached the gravel, and the funnel of twisting air grew firm and tall and dark with whirring particles. Still growing, it advanced toward me. At the last moment it veered to one side, and the flying sand barely stung my legs. As it passed, it devoured a stray piece of newspaper, sucked it up vertically, and then disgorged it. The paper was still floating high in the air when the whirlwind hit the bushes again, lost its vitality, and moved on, diminuendo, toward the river.

The paper sideslipped downward against blue sky, tilting first one way and then the other until it settled beside the truck. It lay for a moment on the gravel. Then a puff of wind lifted one corner and cartwheeled it out of sight.

I sat in the shade beneath the lean-to roof and stared out into the sunlight. For the first time since the customs gate, I felt alone.

An hour before sunset I reached Triple Slash Ranch.

The buildings, dilapidated but belonging, clustered beneath two tall cottonwood trees. The trees cast long shadows onto the buildings, over an open courtyard, and out across a plowed field. Beyond the river, the Arizona hills were still brazen and burning; but there was peace and coming coolness beneath the two cottonwood trees.

I pushed open the gate into the courtyard.

A girl of about seven was towing a toy wagon in wild circles. In the wagon sat a young goat. The girl was sunburnt and blue-eyed and puckish. The goat was brown and semi-cooperative.

As I stepped through the gate, the girl saw me and stopped. The goat looked up gratefully.

"Hullo," I said. "Are Mummy or Daddy at home?"

The girl took a step back.

I was suddenly conscious of being a dirty bearded stranger with a pack and a big stick.

After a moment the girl said, "Yes, Mommy's in the house. But Daddy's out in the fields somewhere."

I knocked on the door of the simple one-story home.

The slight, fair-haired mother refused to take money for the sugar and salt I asked for. And she insisted I accept some oranges. She tried hard to fight down her distrust, but I did not blame her for remembering that "Daddy was out in the fields somewhere."

The girl, holding her mother's hand, suddenly asked, "What do you think I should call my goat please? We only got him today, 'cause my lamb only died yesterday, and I haven't really decided yet."

Her mother smiled.

"I *think* I'll call him Brownie," said the girl with a sort of tentative finality.

The three of us explored the merits of Brownie as a name for a brown goat. Then I asked about campsites. There was a clearing in front of a riverside cabin, two hundred yards up the road.

I fished near the cabin for half an hour, then lit a fire. Soon there were footsteps out in the darkness, and a tall, rangy man came into the outer firelight. The girl from the ranch was holding his hand.

"My wife tells me you're on a long hike," said the man. "I'm just a country boy, but we thought maybe you'd like to come back to the ranch and have supper with us and stay the night in the guest room." He moved closer and the fire lit up his long face. "My name's Ira," he said. "And this is Terry."

The three of us walked back together through the darkness. Just before we reached the ranch house, Terry unburdened her mind. "I think I *will* call him Brownie," she said.

The house was furnished with almost stark simplicity. Everything looked old but spotlessly clean.

Ira was in his early thirties, Corinne a little younger. They had both been grained and thinned by the desert; tempered, but not bent. Both had hung fiercely and proudly onto their grade-school learning and had built onto it a solid practical knowledge of the desert.

Terry was learning too. She explained the habits of different lizards for me, then recited the names of the commoner desert bushes and trees. "And

Mommy says the flowers this year are the best I'll see for a long, long time." Her eyes grew round with wonder. "Maybe for *twenty* years!"

I was surprised when Ira told me that the majestic white birds had been pelicans. One of my earliest memories is of my grandfather reciting:

A wonderful bird is the pelican—
His beak can hold more than his belly can.

And all my life I had thought of pelicans as ugly and comic creatures.

When we sat down to supper, Ira said grace. He blessed the food, then reached out to cover our whole lives. "And give us, Oh Lord, the gift of sincerity . . ."

For supper there was salad, then chicken, then homemade pie. I remembered the last cubes of dehydrated potato in my pack.

During supper I asked about the plump "frontier" cattle I had seen back near Draper and 4S ranches.

"Oh, those are ours," said Ira. "They'll run south for thirty miles, easy. Mostly they stay close to the river, but when the rains are good they range back ten miles and more into the hills. They're devils to find then."

"They're bad enough any time," said Corinne. "I ride out with Ira whenever I can, and those cattle move through the bush as fast as a horse can after a hard day. It gets hot here in summer too—a hundred and ten degrees or more. But it's a good life . . . so long as you don't meet too many rattlers. Oh, you needn't worry, there aren't many about this early in the year."

"What exactly does their rattle sound like?"

"Ooooooh, it sends shivers down your spine," said Corinne. She let one run down, and her shoulders shook.

Ira smiled. "I wouldn't say it was as bad as that, but still . . ."

"Anyway, once you've heard it you'll never forget it," said Corinne.

"And I'm not likely to mistake it?"

"No," said Ira. "You won't mistake it."

After Terry had gone to bed, Ira switched on the radio. The news was mostly about the space race.

"It doesn't seem to matter much out here, does it?" I said, half to myself.

"No," said Ira quietly. "No, it doesn't." Then he looked up sharply. "What has all that got to do with us? All we want is peace and quiet." He sat silent for a moment, staring down at the check tablecloth. "Listen, while you're walking, would you keep an eye open for a place you think might suit us? Close by the river if possible, so's we could irrigate like we do here. There'd have to be some kind of water of course . . ."

"And nobody near," said Corinne.

". . . Just a little place like this where we could be self-sufficient. It used to be quiet down here, but too many people have been coming in these last few years. Now there's all kinds of cabins up the river a little ways, and even a few down below."

I mentioned the black cabin on its acre of bull-dozed gravel.

"Yes, a guy's been trying for years to start up a fishing and hunting resort there. He's just about given up now, I think. . . . Thank God! Still, it shows the way things are going. And it'll get worse. So don't forget—keep an eye open for a place you think we might like."

It was not until I lay half asleep in the guest room in my first bed since Mexico that I grasped, with a rush of comprehension, what I had found at Triple Slash Ranch. I had thought the old frontier ended at the black cabin. And I had expected to get no nearer meeting a frontiersman than I could by daydreaming of an old man living out his last days in a stone house with a view. But the Triple Slash was no ring of stones with a cracked stove outside. It was a living reality. And now Ira and Corinne wanted to do what frontiersmen had always done when advancing civilization caught up with their homesteads: they wanted to push ahead once more and find freedom in the wide and untamed land that still lay ahead.

About ten o'clock next morning I was walking along the Wetback Trail in a rather comatose state, half baked by the sun, when I came around a corner and started back as if I had been kicked in the face.

Across the Trail, five feet ahead, stretched a sinuous brown evilness. As I stumbled back, it rattled. The sound was hard and dry. It began with a rhythm no faster than an outboard motor, then ripped up to a climax so vibrant it was almost a hiss.

I slipped off my pack, opened a camera, and moved forward again.

The snake had not moved. The flat, diamond-shaped head was alert and poised. The eyes were fixed on my bare legs. At intervals a forked tongue flickered out. The neck was a rigid, threatening kink. Behind it, four feet of brown body curved back to the raised rattle.

Breathing hard, I focused the camera from six feet away. Unblinking eyes glared into the viewfinder. When I lowered the camera they fixed again on my bare legs. I felt sweat cold on my spine. There was something actively evil about that sinuous body curved out on the hot rock, about the sense of latent power, about the repulsive beauty of the clean markings. It was an evil that flowed out in pulsating waves.

I put down the camera and picked up my yucca staff.

The snake began to move downhill. It moved slowly, sliding between the rocks with little body motion, its head held rigid and twisted back. Its tongue flickered out toward me. Very softly, it hissed.

Staff held high, I moved up into range. The snake hissed again, louder. Slowly I brought the staff down to within four feet of the ground and held it steady while the snake slid past a rock. At last its head moved out into the open.

I cracked the staff down with all my strength.

The snake convulsed. The staff shattered into fragments. One of them bounced up and hit me over the left eye. When I could see clearly again, the snake was still writhing. I smashed down once more with the stub of the staff. The convulsions redoubled; the stub shattered again. I hurled rocks, one after the other, at the snake's bleeding head. The convulsions lessened, almost ceased.

I sat down on a rock. Now there was time to think, I recognized that when I first stumbled back I had been thrown off balance in more than one sense. I had done exactly the opposite of what I knew was right—stand still until I had made sure the snake was too far away to strike or until it moved out of range. And all the time I was photographing and then killing it I had felt the pulsating waves of evil. But now, sitting safely on a rock and looking at the corpse, I knew they were really waves of fear traveling the other way. I was not proud of the thought.

I also felt rather foolish. One knee was bleeding where I had scraped a rock as I stumbled back. And a lump was forming over my eye.

The snake lay among brown rocks. Its thick brown body was crisscrossed with diamond-shaped markings. The tail tapered to a cigar-shaped stub, ringed by four black-and-white bands like those on a raccoon's tail. The bands were as shiny as if they had been painted on with lacquer enamel. Fixed to the last band was the rattle—a tapering double row of straw-colored beads like a miniature corncob that had been forced to grow flat between two boards.

By the time I had stuck a Band-Aid on my knee, the snake was reviving. Although its head was a battered and bleeding wreck, it began to writhe with new energy. I hurled another rock. It missed. I hurled another. The snake thrashed about in agonized convulsions, then drew into a tight coil and glared at me through clotted blood. Waves of evil flowed out again. I threw more rocks. Even after the head was mere pulp, the body still moved. When I touched its cold scales, the rattle raised a little and buzzed feebly. If I stamped my foot close by, it flicked up and rattled fiercely.

When the snake at last lay still, I measured it with a length of nylon cord. (Later it checked at forty-six inches.) Then I held it up by the battered head and took a self-portrait. Finally I cut off the twelve-bead rattle.*

When at last I walked on down the Wetback Trail toward Palo Verde, I felt as if I had survived a desert initiation ceremony.

For a hundred miles beyond Palo Verde, man had part-tamed the Colorado and its desert.

Palo Verde Valley itself had been subjugated: orchards and fields ruled the plain into a green checkerboard. But beyond the irrigation I walked through a once-over-lightly-with-gasoline-and-playthings desert.

A highway paralleled the Colorado. Every eight or ten miles there was a gas station, a cafe, or a fishing camp. And up and down the river sped brightly painted boats, prickly with fishing rods.

Because of my Death Valley deadline, I hurried north for almost sixty miles along the paved highway. Along the highway, man's works were thinly spread, leaving long stretches of country almost untouched. But I rarely felt in contact with the desert. The veneer of civilization seemed to seal it

---

*Desert custom dictates that you register victory in terms of rattles. Every bead means a year's growth, the reasoning goes, so the more beads a snake has to its rattle, the older and more dangerous it must be.

Much later, I discovered that this was part of the dense myth cloud that surrounds rattlesnakes. On the rare occasions that a rattle is complete, the number of beads does in fact show how often the snake has shed its skin. But the number of times a snake has shed gives no accurate indication of its age. And age is no guide at all to formidability quotient.

off. And as I walked I found that I was looking at our civilization from a new, excluded point of view.

Two weeks earlier I had driven south along this same highway. Then, the car had wafted us along in cushioned privacy. Now, cars were monsters that snarled past, tearing the air. They left a dusty, tainted aftertaste.

The journey south had left me with no clear memory of the country. Outside the car window, the desert had passed like a badly focused filmstrip, mile after monotonous mile. It had little scent and no texture. But now, on foot, I was in touch with those vital details that turn mere landscape into living countryside. Butterflies flickered like kaleidoscopes. Grasshoppers filled the air. One moment I was in a hothouse; the next, a mountain breeze blew cool on my cheek. I walked toward a dark roadside patch that to a motorist would be one blur among thousands; it focused into a wreath of purple flowers. A brown blob off the left became a fat barrel cactus that, like a woman conscious of her girth, wore its spines in severe vertical stripes. And the distance moved closer. Mountains passed slowly, like distant ships; I could savor each change of outline, each subtle change of color.

But even on foot the highway held the desert at arm's length. The road itself kept stalking along on stilts or grubbing about in a trough. My feet trod on harsh and sterile pavement.

The moment I struck off the highway I found myself back "in" the desert. A long-legged lizard scurried for cover, kicking up little spurts of dust as it cornered around a bush. Muddy hollows, baked hard after rain, had cracked into intricate mosaics. Bees droned above beds of yellow flowers. The flowers themselves grew so thick that my boots were soon yellow with pollen.

The second morning, a passing motorist screeched to a halt and offered me a ride.

When I declined, he pushed back his hat. "But what the heck d'you want to *walk* through this wilderness for?"

"Well, there's always something to see," I said. I pointed back along the road. "This year, the flowers are enough by themselves."

"Flowers?" said the motorist. "*What* flowers?"

But the people who actually lived in this part-tamed desert often knew a great deal about what went on around them.

I met Mr. Tuttle in a roadside cafe. He was tall and scraggy, about sixty-five. He came in carrying a long bamboo stick with a wire loop at one end. When he saw my pack he modified his morose, hawk-like expression.

"Along the river? You must have passed Triple Slash Ranch then."

"Sure, I stayed the night with Ira and Corinne."

"Did you now? Quite a man, that Ira. I remember they caught him once taking five wetbacks into Palo Verde in his car. Arrested him and took him up in front of the judge. 'You know,' says the judge, 'I could give you twenty years for this.' 'I know,' says Ira. 'But they were just men like you and me, only hungry and thirsty. And the valley's full of them.' They let him go in the end—'Because the valley's full of them,' the judge said."

Mr. Tuttle was a rattlesnake expert. He had even been bitten. "But that was twenty years back," he said rolling his pants leg back down over the scar on his calf. "I was green then." He demonstrated how he slipped the wire loop on his stick over a snake's body. "The stick gives me plenty of room for safety," he said. "You'll read that a rattler can strike two-thirds of its length. Maybe that's right, but I doubt it. More like half of its length. But they can strike from any position; they don't have to coil, like some people think. And remember, they'll never attack. They're more frightened than you are. They may come toward you, but that'll be for some other reason, likely because it's downhill."

I mentioned how my rattler had revived after I felt sure it was dead.

"Yes," said Mr. Tuttle. "I've held this wire loop tight around one's neck for half an hour and thrown it aside as dead, and then had it start crawling off five minutes later. You've got to pound that head real flat. But if you can't get at the head—if it's under a bush or something—break its back. Just hit it across the body, near the tail if you can, where it's weakest. It can't do much after that. Once it realizes it's more than just wounded, it'll often bite itself. It doesn't take long to die then."

Mr. Tuttle had done his share of reading too. He told me of an experiment in which two balloons—one filled with hot air, one with cold—had been lowered repeatedly into a captive rattler's cage. The snake always struck the hot one.

"Heat bulbs in the head," explained Mr. Tuttle.

Rattlesnake venom, he said, lasted for years. A certain rancher in that area had one day worn a pair of his father's knee boots that he found in a cupboard. The father had been dead ten years, but the boots were still in good shape. Next day the rancher's leg began to swell. It rapidly grew worse.

Eventually he went to a doctor—just in time to avoid amputation. The doctor diagnosed rattlesnake venom. The rancher said he had not so much as seen a snake for months. Then he remembered that his father had been struck when wearing the same boots a year before he died. The doctor came to the conclusion that one of the snake's poisonous fangs must have broken off and lodged in an eyehole. Eleven years later it had scratched the son. Afterward it must have fallen out.

"Are there any other poisonous snakes around here?" I asked Mr. Tuttle.

"Not snakes, no. But there's a few black widow spiders. They're quite small, with round bodies hardly as big as a marble. All black, except for a red patch shaped like an hourglass under the body. Nasty things. But you don't see them too often. They mostly keep to dark places."

"Anything else?"

"Well, there's supposed to be Gila monsters. But they're mighty rare. I've never seen one myself. Rattlers are really the only things you've got to look for."

"And I can be pretty sure any snake that's not a rattler is harmless?"

"Yes. But don't forget rattlers can lose their rattles. There aren't many other snakes around here anyways, except maybe desert racers. They're quite harmless. Long thin things, bright red. They can really move. You've got to run at a fair pace to keep up with them. If you stop and run back the other way, they'll sometimes turn around and come right after you. Then you stop and run back toward them, and off they go again. And so on. I've had a lot of fun with them like that." Mr. Tuttle laughed quietly. His long face creased into a pattern that finally eliminated the morose, hawk-like look.

"Have you always lived around here?" I asked.

"Oh no, only four and a half years. But I like it here. I've got a little place close by where nobody bothers me." He glanced around to make sure no one could hear. "Up there I see all the wildlife I want to. Why, every day I feed a hundred quail and rabbits right by my front door."

Soon afterward, Mr. Tuttle got up to go. As we shook hands he said, "When you get another staff, try for Calcutta cane. Don't settle for less than semi-solid bamboo. And bind it with adhesive tape as soon as it starts to dry out. Otherwise it'll splinter. Well, I hope the hike goes well . . . and I hope I've been some sort of help."*

---

*Many months later I recognized that Mr. Tuttle was as much a desert phenomenon as his rattlesnakes. For the shifting myth cloud that swirls around rattlers has its constants, and they are perpetuated by a well-defined group of retailers. Acute observers like Mr. Tuttle will purvey, along with accurate first-hand information, legends that have been handed down for generations.

One of them is the idea that wounded rattlers will commit suicide by biting themselves. They may thrash around, striking at random, and bite themselves by mistake, but that is all. Animals other than man almost certainly cannot comprehend death, let alone reason out ways of inflicting it on themselves. In any case, rattlers are highly immune to their own venom.

The Legend of the Fatal Boot is one of the most persistent in all rattlesnake lore. Laurence Klauber, in his "bible" on the subject, *Rattlesnakes*, reports that the story appears in a paper read to the Royal Society of London in 1714. Then, the fatalities occurred to three successive husbands in Virginia. As frontier and folklore moved west, the story mutated but gained in vigor. Today it flourishes in a hundred forms. But the amount of venom that can be retained on a rattlesnake fang is negligible; and venom exposed to air quickly loses its toxicity.

Twice in the next two days I had cause to remember Mr. Tuttle.

First, there was the rattlesnake.

It rattled at me (or perhaps at a passing Cadillac) as I walked along the highway next morning. It was a size larger all 'round than my first, and evil pulsated out from it almost as strongly. As it slid toward me down a gravel bank, I quoted to myself, "Rattlers never attack. They may come toward you, but that'll be for some other reason, likely because it's downhill." Then I moved aside. The snake seemed to head for my pack, which I had slipped off and left in the sun. Remembering "heat bulbs in the head" and "venom can last for years," I moved the pack out of range. The snake took cover in a creosote bush, leaving a few inches of tail outside. I cut a stick and smashed it down, as high on the body as I could. A head emerged from the bush and waved feebly. That was all. I had meant to see if the snake bit itself, but the poor creature looked so pitiful and helpless that I quickly battered its head flat.

Second, there was the "mirage."

The highway looped far back from the Colorado, and I had taken a ten-mile shortcut across a barren brown mesa that bordered the river. About four o'clock I saw a line of brilliant greenery quivering low in the heat haze ahead.

"A mirage!" I thought. "A genuine mirage!"

Half an hour later I was walking beside a field of very tangible barley, green and thick, and rustling like taffeta.

Outside the barley, close to a shallow irrigation ditch, the sandy soil had cracked into deep fissures. A black spider with a body about the size of a marble scuttled away from my boot. I knelt down and peered at it. The spider angled down into a fissure. As it tilted over I glimpsed a red patch on the underside of its body. It was shaped like an hourglass.

Beyond the barley, outside a row of big new barns, I found the ranch manager.

"Sure it would be a black widow," he said. "Any number of the damned things around here."

"I thought they only lived in dark places."

"All I know is that here they don't seem to care where they go. Usually they don't trouble you, but some times of year they're deadly. I was standing out in that same field once with some Mexicans when one of them brushed his arm as if he was being tickled by something. Then he shook a black widow out of his sleeve. Within minutes the guy passed clean out. Luckily there was a doctor staying on the ranch. We had him there real quick, and he brought the man 'round all right. He was sick for a while, but nothing too bad. The doc said that if he hadn't happened to be there the man could easy have died."*

The manager was understandably proud of his ranch. "Six years ago," he said, "this was just another stretch of mesa. Flatter than most maybe—that's why we bought it. But no different otherwise. And now we've got three hundred acres of the finest citrus and barley and alfalfa along the Colorado."

"But where does the water come from?" I asked.

---

*A friend of mine who makes something of a study of desert lore was delighted to hear of this conversation. "You may not have picked up much accurate information about black widows," he said. "But you certainly learned something about the imaginative powers of Mexican laborers, doctors, and/or ranch managers."

The ranch seemed too high above the river for ordinary irrigation.

"Wells," said the manager. "All from wells. We pump every drop of it. Makes it expensive of course; last year was the first time we showed a profit. But now everybody's sitting up and taking notice. All the land 'round about has been bought up and they're just waiting to see what happens. If we make a real go of it we could change the whole face of the desert. That's about the size of it—change the whole face of the desert."

I walked on through an orchard. The air felt cool and moist. My feet sank into soft earth. In untilled corners, grass grew thick.

Then the trees ended and I stepped back into untamed desert.

The breeze hit me like the blast from a hair dryer. My feet crunched over stones and gravel. The sunlight bounced up like something solid. Ahead, creosote bushes shimmered endlessly away to blue hills.

Twenty minutes later I stopped to look back. The ranch had sunk to a quivering line of green along the flat brown horizon.

Any man in his senses would have dismissed it as a mirage.

Next day I discovered that the part-tamed desert still harbored the genus "desert rat." Within a couple of hours I met two genuine specimens.

Chickenhouse Smith lived under a tamarisk tree. He was a very ordinary-looking man in his mid-fifties, conventionally dressed. Only his house hinted at genius. It had no roof except the branches of the tamarisk tree. Stacked wooden crates contributed two walls and an affluence of built-in cupboards.

They enclosed, very vaguely, a bed, half a dozen chairs, two tables, two refrigerators, a dog, and several electric light bulbs sprouting from an overhead cable. "Outside" stood a vintage Packard coupe.

"I've got homes like this clear across the desert," said Chickenhouse Smith. "Five or six of them."

We strolled "out" into the desert, and he showed me how to tell one tree from another. After the trees we went on to bushes. By the time we started on the flowers his voice was soft and lyrical.

But he had no romantic illusions about the desert.

"Crossing the Mojave, huh?" he said. He scooped a copy of *Life* magazine from one of his built-in cupboards, flipped the pages, and handed it to me, open. A low-level air photograph showed a corpse spread-eagled on glaring sand. A bicycle lay nearby. The caption read: "Mojave Desert claims another victim."

"No hat," said Chickenhouse Smith. "And no water, likely. But just be careful and you'll be all right. If I was you now, I'd make darned sure somebody always knew my schedule, like you say those Border Patrol guys did. And remember, don't try to fight the desert. Just learn to get along with it."

Five miles up the road I came to a tumbledown old building that might once have been a store. Its unpainted walls were cracked and sagging. The windows had grown opaque with dirt. As I walked past I saw dimly, through a glass panel of the door, a cardboard sign that said OPEN—WALK IN.

I turned the handle and pushed. The door opened.

"Come right in," called an old woman's voice from a back room. "Come right in."

I stepped inside.

A wasted figure hobbled out of the back room. A shriveled old man's face peered at me. It was half hidden behind a bulbous gray beard.

"Do you by any chance stock bamboo walking staffs?" I asked.

" 'Fraid not," said the old man in his old woman's voice. "Nothing like it . . . But how'd you like a cup o' coffee?"

"Well, I don't actually want any coffee, thanks . . . but I wonder if I could change film in here, out of the sun?"

"Sure," piped the old man. "Sure. Take your pack off and sit down." He hobbled past me and sat down on a narrow bed. "Black-and-white film?" he asked as I opened the camera.

"No, there's color in this camera, black-and-white in the other."

"Oh," said the the old man.

I took out a little lens brush with a gold-plated case that I had often fooled people into believing was a lipstick. I hesitated, wondering whether to play the lipstick joke on the old man.

"What's that you got there?" he asked sharply.

"Well, it's really a camel's-hair brush for cleaning camera lenses, but . . ."

"Looks more like a lipstick to me," cackled the old man. He rocked back on the bed, his thin body shaking.

I dusted out the camera. Once, I looked up and found the old man staring at me. His legs dangled over the edge of the bed. The ankles were thin, almost deformed. His hands were gnarled and shriveled, as if from arthritis.

"How old are you?" he asked suddenly.

"Thirty-six."

"Hmph, when I was thirty-six I had a better beard than that . . . Where d'you come from?"

"Well . . . England."

"New England, eh? Thought it must be somewhere like that. Way you talk sounds gibberish to me. How long since you left New England?"

"Well, er . . . England, not New England. In fact, to be accurate, Wales."

"Oh . . . My grandfather came from Scotland."

"Oh yes? What part?"

"Don't know. Just know he came from Scotland." The old man sat silent again.

I fumbled in my pack for a film.

"Can't understand why you carry a great pack like that. Why, when I was a young man I didn't pack nothing but a blanket in the desert. And I'd walk sixty miles on a pint of water. But you young fellows these days don't know how to walk. Even go along with your mouths open. 'Course you get thirsty. When *I* walked I'd never open my mouth all day. Just sucked a pebble, a little smooth pebble the size of a bean. That stops you getting thirsty all right. But you young fellows can't do it no more. A little pebble the size of a bean, that's all you need. Why, I've walked clear across the Mojave before now . . ."

"Is it bad snake country, up in the Mojave?"

"Bad snake country? No such thing as bad snake country. Rattlers is all right if you treat 'em right. Handled 'em for years in show business, I did. Used to sit in a pit with 'em crawling all over me—'round my waist and shoulders and everywhere. No such thing as bad snake country, I tell you. Just treat 'em right, that's all . . . Ever been in Canada?"

"Yes, I was up there for a while."

"How long?"

"Three years."

"*I* was there for five." The old man leaned back on the bed and yawned copiously.

I closed the camera, feeling sorry we had failed so completely to understand each other. I stood up and hung the camera on my pack. "Well, thanks a lot for letting me change the film indoors," I said. "Is there anywhere near here I *might* get a bamboo staff?"

The old man suddenly seemed sorry too. "Sure there is. Sure there is. Guy lives in a trailer down by the river. Don't know what he wants bamboos for, but he keeps a whole stack." He hobbled to the door and pointed out the way. "Say, that's a mighty good-looking pack you've got there. Pretty heavy too. Still, I guess you're used to it by now. Well, good-bye . . . and good luck."

I walked slowly down toward the river.

The man in the trailer refused to accept payment for a bamboo staff. "Glad to give it to you," he said. "And I hope you get a rattler with it. One of them killed my brother."

I asked him about the old man in the store.

"That's Frenchy Buchanan," he said. "I'm afraid he's a lonely old fellow these days. Doesn't do much anymore. He takes some beautiful color photographs though."

I was still wondering when I said good-bye. "Frenchy Buchanan . . ." I said. "His hands and legs . . . has he got arthritis?"

The man hesitated just a second. "No," he said. "He was nearly beaten to death a year or two back. Shot a man's dog."

Almost at the end of the part-tamed desert I came to Earp. It was one of man's early Colorado projects.

Two highways met. Together, they crossed a railroad and the river. A dozen trees commemorated these events.

As I walked down the railroad track I saw a gray water tank floating blimpishly above the trees. On its side was painted:

WYATT
EARP
HOME

The water tank dominated the village. It was strategically sited to attract the eye of every northbound motorist, and appreciably increased his chances of misjudging the curve and crashing into the corrugated iron

EARP TRADING POST
Cold Beer—Ice Live Bait
Fishing Tackle Groceries

The motorist's final prospect as he pierced the wall of the trading post would be the legend that ran its entire length:

WELCOME TO EARP, CALIFORNIA

Beyond the trading post, the garage lurked behind a pageant of billboards. The biggest proclaimed:

THIS TOWN NAMED
FOR WYATT EARP
EARLY FRONTIER MARSHALL
of TV series.

Another sign added, just to make sure:

EARP, CALIF.

Beyond the garage stood the post office and a line of frame cabins collectively labeled "Motel."

Earp slept.

A heat mirage wavered up from the highway. Only on the veranda of the trading post was there shade. No vehicle, no person, marred the peace. No TV aerial corrupted the skyline. If it had not been for the TV postscript to the garage proclamation, you could have imagined the Earpians to be so far behind the times that they imagined Wyatt Earp was still dead.

But when I left next evening, Earp no longer dozed in the sun.

All day, rain had threatened. Now, heavy clouds were rolling up from the south. Fierce squalls whipped bulging screens of dust between the buildings. For some reason I was feeling mildly depressed, and the weather fitted my mood.

When I took the key of my cabin to the old woman who kept the motel, she stood in the doorway and wrapped her scarf more tightly about her. "For Heaven's sakes!" she said. "Surely you're not going tonight? Not in this weather?"

"Oh yes," I said. "I'll make five or six miles this evening."

"You'll be sorry after half a mile. It'll be raining any minute now. And this is a high wind for here. Lifting roofs off. I'd no more think of going out than I would flying."

"Oh, I'll be all right. I was born lucky."

The woman weighed the key in her hand. "You can have the cabin for three dollars tonight," she said.

I thanked her but declined.

"You'll be sorry after half a mile," she said again. "Wait 'til you get down the road a ways . . . you'll be sorry after half a mile."

The wind helped me on my way. The gusts had fused into a steady gale that funneled up the valley and caught my pack like a sail. The gale drew the desert closer, stripping away the thin veneer of civilization. Stinging particles of sand flew along the road. Scents chased one after another down the wind.

The light was failing when a car pulled up beside me, closed tight against my world of freshness and effort. A window slid down and I found myself looking along a sumptuous, chrome-filled dash. Cigarette smoke hung in warped blue layers. The radio billed and cooed. It was like the first moment inside a nightclub.

The driver leaned away from the weather. "Ride?" he asked.

Gently, I refused.

The man looked shocked. "Christ!" he said. "Never heard anybody say 'no' to a ride before." He pressed a button and the window slid up. The car moved on.

It began to rain. A few huge, tentative drops, then a steady downpour. The wind wrapped my poncho around me and bowled me along the road. The sting of rain on bare legs refreshed without hurting.

Darkness fell.

Headlights approached obliquely, then swept 'round through an arc of weeping bushes. The beam impaled me. The motor faltered, then picked up again. The car flashed past, slicing the wind and flinging cold spray. I paused to reaccustom my eyes to the darkness; then the wet pavement showed faintly and I could let the wind carry me along again.

The rain grew heavier and washed the desert even cleaner. The scents magnified. I began to sing—popular hits, bawdy wartime songs, an exultant theme from Brahms' First Symphony, any tune that was loud and triumphant enough to shout at the darkness. The darkness accepted them all. It snatched them out of my mouth and flung them away down the road with a joyful cry that it disguised only thinly as the sound of wind tearing through bushes and rain lashing against wet earth.

By the time I saw the lights of a roadside cafe, I had been walking through the darkness for an hour, and the somber mood in which I left Earp had been swept headlong before the wind and rain.

Inside the warm cafe, the storm was only a futile pattering of rain on windows. By the time I finished dinner, the pattering had stopped, and I went back to the desert.

The clouds were breaking up. Soon the stars began. And by the time I had picked some branches for a bed and shaken the water from them and rolled out my sleeping bag, the stars had filled the sky and thrown a shower of gems into the dark bushes that stood sentinel around my bedroom.

Beyond Parker Dam I walked out into open desert again.

It was only sixty miles now to Needles, where I would strike away from the Colorado. Most of the way, man had hardly penetrated. The river would once more be my lifeline.

But the river was no longer a river. Held back by Parker Dam, the water had spread up and out until a lake stretched three miles and more across to the Arizona mountains. Far out on its pewter surface, powerboats sometimes drew tiny white smudges. But they did not disturb the solitude; the sweep of land and water absorbed them into insignificance. Occasionally, from far overhead, the roar of jet aircraft floated down. But, alone once more with the desert, miles from any sign of man, I heard them as if through a mute. They were unreal, not quite believable.

Apart from the lake, the desert was very like "the old frontier" below Palo Verde; but I kept finding novelties in it. At first I put the sense of newness down to a change in the weather. For several days, gray cloud pressed down and a cold wind blew. When the wind dropped, the clouds discarded a little moisture with such languor that rain seemed too harsh a word. The rain and cold at least stopped me worrying about rattlesnakes; every "expert" had told me that this early in the year they came out only on the hottest days. On the coldest day of all, within twenty minutes, I met and killed two more rattlesnakes.

When the clouds broke up and the sun shone once more, the desert still had something novel about it. I seemed to see and hear and smell and feel it more vividly than before. I watched scurrying beetles and felt compassion for them when they reminded me of Wall Street automatons, motivated by ticker tapes. I laughed when a turquoise-breasted hummingbird introduced itself, curtsying, six inches from my nose. When a brown flash darted away in front of me and disappeared into a house of many patios, weathered in the wall of a rock gully, I sat waiting with camera in hand until out onto one of the patios came first a whiskered nose that wrinkled and sniffed, then a furry head that peered, and finally the body and twitchety tail of a neat brown ground squirrel that frisked out of his house and nibbled away at a purple flower in the front garden. And when I walked on again I found myself reveling with almost no guilt in the criminal and delightful opulence of brushing aside flowers with my feet, step after step, hour after hour, day after day.

Soon, man's last tracks petered out and there were only wild burro trails to follow. I climbed into the foothills of a massif that promised the finest river scenery so far, and the bluffs and canyons and crags grew steeper and closer together until finally even the burro trails petered out. And all at once, for no particular reason, I realized that I was appreciating the desert more keenly because I had time to stand and stare. I had thrown off the frustrating urgency that so plagued me back along "the old frontier." I had mastered the concrete problems at last. The shakedown cruise was really over.

The food problem no longer ate up hours of every day. I had evolved a simple, practical, basic, dehydrated menu:

Breakfast—4 ounces fruit; tea.
Lunch—1½ ounces powdered soup; tea.
Britannic afternoon tea—tea.
Supper—4 ounces potatoes, 2 ounces pemmican; also, sometimes up to 2 ounces vegetables.

Dry cereal and chocolate varied the diet. At hourly halts I munched raisins and high-calorie mintcake (a candy popular with mountaineering and polar expeditions). Two ounces of it, used as a between-meals reviver, saw me through the longest day. By now I knew just how much food to order for a given "leg" (at about 2¼ pounds a day), and a package would be waiting at each post office.

Kitchen technique had ceased to be a time-consuming monster too. Kitchen utensils consisted of a stainless steel Sierra Club cup, a spoon, a sheath knife that did every job from gutting fish to splitting kindling, and two nesting aluminum-alloy cooking pots with lids that doubled as plates or pans. The two pots weighed just 1 pound 4 ounces, but they were tough. Once, the large one bounded 150 feet down a talus slope and suffered nothing more than a couple of small dents.

By now I was managing the kitchen like a master chef. I could even cook after dark and let my mind wander off onto other things. But I was still learning details. Learning the hard way. Sugar and detergent at first lived in identical square plastic boxes.

Then, one sleepy pre-sunrise breakfast, I sprinkled my fruit with a thick, soapy coating. One of the first things I bought at Earp was a small plastic bottle for the detergent.

The other domestic duties no longer kept my mind on a treadmill.

At night camps I wasted no time circling around like a dog stirred by ancestral memories. I could recognize a good site at a glance: a flat bedroom; creosote bushes for a mattress; firewood; and a bathroom. The bathroom most of all. There is a yawning gap between a camp with running bedside water and one from which you have to crash through bushes, tules, and ankle-deep swamp to reach a tepid out-puddle of the river. By comparison, the difference between hotel rooms with and without a private bath is so much fiddle-faddle.

I was a little surprised to find, when I came to consider it, that some of the inconsequential routine chores were now minor but distinct pleasures. Taking off socks for example. In everyday life, the act usually passes unnoticed; now, peeling them off at night camp was sheer delight. Afterward, pemmican and dehydrated potato tasted better than any caviar. And my tiredness as I slid into the sleeping bag was as far removed from the exhaustion after a long drive as a waltz is from St. Vitus' Dance.

One of the things that had helped my new appreciation of the desert was a change in water-drinking habits. At first I had followed the old spartan routine of no water between meals. That way, thirst rarely became an actual physical discomfort, but sometimes I walked for hours with my mind covered by a kind of dehydrated scum that blocked out the subtleties of the desert. After Earp I tried sipping water at almost every halt. It washed away the scum and honed the edge of my appreciation.

By now I trusted the equipment too. The pack was my friend and comfort—a house on my back. The welded aluminum frame let air circulate freely around my spine, and I had learned how to adjust the straps so that the load was shared by the foam-padded yoke on my shoulders and a taut nylon band on my hips. I doubt if there is such a thing as a permanently waterproof pack bag, but the impregnated fabric that mine was made of brought it about as close as you can get. Repacking the bag was by now more or less automatic. Everything had its place—with variations: I knew what I would need next, and that went in last. Certain items were always ready to hand: the flashlight for example (with batteries turned back-to-back to prevent accidental switching on), and the toilet paper (in rolls, not interleaved packs that in a wind flew apart like bombs). And I had learned the value of plastic food bags for holding almost anything from toilet gear, through camp moccasins, to smoky cooking pots. But the most surprising thing about my pack was the affection I felt for it. As long as I carried it, home was where I happened to be.

The bedroom was my down-filled mummy bag (weighing 5 pounds 10 ounces and contoured to take a human body rather than a small upright piano). Sleeping naked, I had yet to feel cold in it. No sleeping bag can be waterproof of course (in cold weather you would freeze in your own moisture). The cover of my bag was made of Egyptian cotton and labeled "water-repellant"—a term that fills me with distrust: like "Hi-Fi" or "psychosomatic," it can mean almost anything—or almost nothing. But the bag actually repelled water. A shower might soak the outer cover, but inside I would snuggle dry as a dehydrated potato.

At the start, because I was city soft, I had carried a 2-pound plastic mattress. I didn't expect it to last long, and it didn't. From the fifth day onward I spread foliage under my bed. Within a day or two I was sleeping just as comfortably. And I was thankful to be carrying 2 pounds less.

On the whole, my decisions about weight had turned out well. For example, my two cameras (35-mm and folding 2¼ inches) together weighed only 3 pounds 10 ounces, the poncho 1 pound 3 ounces, and a folding can opener ⅛ of an ounce. The only items on which I had not pared away at half-ounces were water canteens. In the desert, the safety of your water outweighs all other considerations. My three half-gallon canteens—all aluminum, with screw tops—weighed 13 ounces each. But they were tough, and I trusted them.

Backpacking is not only a matter of pounds on the back. The successful 1953 Everest expedition established that in terms of physical effort 1 pound on the feet is equivalent to 5 on the shoulders. But I had known that my boots would have to stand up to tough going. As a compromise, I had chosen six-inch Italian mountaineering boots weighing 3 pounds 10 ounces. Rubber padding in the uppers made them very easy to break in but rather warm in the desert.

The boots themselves had turned out well. The uppers, kept well waxed, were still in good shape. And the non-slip Vibram lug soles had worn very little. I am heavy on heels though, and I was glad

I had mailed a spare pair ahead with the maps to Needles, my next post office. (Two days later, in Needles, I was waiting for the heels to be fitted when I met a surveyor who said he had never found a boot that would last more than two months in the kind of country I had come through. He turned one of mine over in his hand. "Hmph," he said. "Almost as good as new.")

But, right from the start, I had run into insole trouble. The very first day, the soles of my feet had been chafed by protruding hand stitching. The only insoles I had been able to buy at a little store near the border had been foam rubber. They had turned out to be intolerably hot. Substitutes cut from cereal boxes last about six hours. Later, I had bought asbestos gasket sheeting from a wayside garage and cut insoles to insulate the foam rubber. This was an improvement, but no final answer. Soon I could manage fifteen miles a day with reasonable comfort, but sore feet still tended to limit the mileage. (Later still, I glued in wholly satisfactory leather insoles.)

A regular fifteen miles a day was the target I had set myself for the Mojave Desert. At Needles I would be cutting away from my Colorado lifeline and striking due west. Each day across the Mojave I would have to move from water to water (springs, wells, human habitations, or whatever offered). For safety I would have to carry extra water. And any physical inefficiency or equipment failure would mean trouble. But now I felt fit and competent. I could hardly claim yet that I was as much at home in the desert as I had been in my apartment; but I no longer felt like a scorpion on the seabed.

All this meant I could plan ahead more confidently. By now, I knew my walking rates fairly accurately. Along roads I covered three miles in the hour, including a ten-minute rest. Cross-country, I rarely managed more than two miles. Over really rough desert the average sometimes fell to less than half a mile. But to incorporate these figures into an estimate of a day's journey required not so much a grasp of arithmetic as an understanding of human frailty. Seven hours' walking a day does not sound much. But put a fifty-pound pack on your back and walk through desert that teems with attractions and you will begin to understand. The temptations to dillydally are about as easy to evade as hydrogen bombs. Days repeatedly atomize:

	Hours	*Minutes*
Walking, including ten-minute halts every hour	7	—
Extension of half the ten-minute halts to twenty minutes because of flowers, inertia, or views from old stone houses	—	30
Compulsive dallying for photography and general admiration of the desert—$4\frac{2}{7}$ minutes in every hour	—	30
Photography, once a day, of a difficult and utterly irresistible object. (This will seem a gross overestimate to nonphotographers; an absurd underestimate to the initiated)	1	—
Conversations with rattlesnake experts, desert rats, and desert ground squirrels	1	—
Cooking and consumption of four meals, including tea	3	30
Camp chores	—	30

	Hours	*Minutes*
Orthodox business of wilderness traveler: rapt contemplation of nature and/or navel.	—	30
Evaporated time, quite unaccountable for	—	30
Sleep (and you need it)	8	59
Reading, fishing, additional rest, elevated thinking, unmentionable items, and general sloth	—	1
Total:	24	—

In other words, although the shakedown cruise was finally over, I had still not quite managed to throw off our modern habit of hurry.

The Colorado kept its finest spectacle until the end.

Since Parker Dam I had walked in solitude; but almost all the way there had been signs of man. For a few miles above the dam he had begun to tame the desert, and I followed a dirt track that served two fishing camps. Beyond the track there had been wild burro trails and, although I never saw any burros, their trumpeting often sounded nearby (and while wild burros roam only where man does not, they come from man-raised stock). But as I followed the river into the foothills of a mountain block, even the burro trails petered out. And the Colorado, which ever since Parker Dam had been a man-made lake, became a river again, swirling once more in turbid freedom. As I climbed into the heart of the mountains I saw that at last I had found a corner of the river and its desert that man had not even tried to tame. This was somebody else's kingdom.

I climbed a crag in the crook of the Devil's Elbow and looked down into His hideout.

Since time began He had been searing the rock white hot, cooling it, then searing it again, until now it threatened to crumble before the next puff of wind. Parched red peaks thrust up from a wilderness of writhing ridges. Brassy sunlight laid bare every tortured shape, every layered slash of brown and slate and sickly green. Dante would have known the place.

Through the center of this huge desiccation, a thousand feet below me, sliced the Colorado. Twice within a mile it pivoted in elbows that sent whorls careering across its surface. At the canyon walls, blue water brushed past burning rock. Beyond the river, rock pinnacles mounted one above the other in colossal anarchy.

I sat all morning on the crag. Once, a powerboat passed down the river. It was a silent, insignificant speck.

Northward, the way I was going, the mountains fell away into a broad plain. Beyond the plain, the way I would not be going, rose more mountains. Somewhere among them—contestable as it seemed in my sunlit silence—stood the casinos of Las Vegas.

Camp that night was my last beside the Colorado.

It began well when a promontory I had selected from the map yielded every advantage I had hoped for. (There is a peculiar satisfaction about choosing a really good campsite from the map; you get the same slightly surprised pleasure as from finding that your checkbook total tallies with the bank statement.)

After supper I sat beside a dying fire, listening to the back eddy that swirled beside my promontory. It rose and fell with unsteady rhythm in response to some subtle pulse of the main river. The moon levered itself free of the Arizona mountains and flooded the desert with silver light.

But the night was still dark and mysterious, and when a large fish jumped clear of the water, so close that I half expected to feel the spray, I saw nothing. The fish jumped again, farther away. Then it circled the back eddy, jumping again and again at intervals of about a minute. I peered into the silver darkness, half-consciously counting the jumps. The tenth sounded close again, but still I could see nothing. Twice more the fish circled the back eddy. Then it swung out into the main river. The sounds of its splashes came back through the night, fainter and fainter, until they merged at last with the sound of the Colorado. The final jump was number twenty-nine.

I rolled out my sleeping bag and went contentedly to sleep.

In the middle of the night I woke to hear the jumping sound again. The fish circled the back eddy once, jumping at regular intervals. Then it too swung out into the main river. The sound tapered off downstream until at last there was only the river talking to the night. Listening and remembering, I felt that for the first time I shared a secret with the river. There was an innocent schoolboy excitement about it, like the secret of your first luminous watch under the bedclothes. And lying there in the moonlight, half asleep, I felt at last the beginnings of affection for the Colorado—an affection I feel for nearly all rivers. Its voice still muttered threats; but I was no longer afraid, only respectful. For more than two hundred miles the river had been my lifeline and a boundary of my world. Gradually, without my noticing, it had become other things as well. It had kept me company, often sharing the days and nights with no one. And it had given me memories: sunsets and pelicans and people, and now fish that jumped in the night.

As I let myself sink back to sleep, I felt sad at the thought of leaving it. And, remembering the fish, I seemed to hear in its splashes a hint of why I was walking up California, a hint of those "reasons," more worthwhile than "discovering America," that I knew The Walk would show me in the end.

By ten o'clock next morning I could see a bridge and the black slash of a highway cutting across the desert. Soon I made out other structures. When I came up level I found, crowded together in half a mile of river, a road bridge and a rail bridge and three structures carrying natural-gas pipelines. Their sweeping latticeworks shone red and black and silver in the desert sunlight, as pleasing in themselves as a well-designed industrial plant. But even while I admired them I found myself looking back at the pinnacles that soared up around the Devil's Elbow. Ever since Mexico I had, without altogether realizing it, been on the side of the river in its struggle against man. Now, with the beginnings of affection for it, I saw quite clearly where my sympathies lay. And these bridges carried new threats. They stated with cold finality what I had been hiding from myself: that although man might move slowly, and might sometimes be repulsed, he would in the end be able to tame every yard of the Colorado and its desert. It was inevitable, a part of the onward flow of evolution. But evolution is full of built-in stabilizers, and there would always be forces striving to conserve for posterity a few unspoiled corners of America. The Colorado had made me understand the need for such conservation, made me feel it deep in my bones instead of merely in the confines of my brain. And I was, perhaps, more grateful to it for this revelation than for anything else.

I turned my back on the bridges at last and began to walk northward along the highway. It was the "Route 66" of the song. Soon a railroad track offered a shortcut, and before long I came singing into Needles along the Atchison, Topeka and Santa Fe. On the way south, I had driven from Needles to the Mexican border in four hours. The return journey had taken exactly four weeks.

In Needles I paused. But Death Valley was still 150 miles away; and, if I was to keep on schedule, I had only ten days in which to reach there. Soon, I hurried westward up a slow but steady slope, away from the river that had been my lifeline and out into the Mojave Desert.

CHAPTER

3

ACROSS THE MOJAVE

The Mojave Desert has an evil reputation. All over the West, its name conjures up a picture of scorched and empty wilderness, implacably hostile to man. "The Mojave claims *another* victim," Chickenhouse Smith's magazine had said. And back in San Francisco a friend had stared at me openmouthed: "My God! Across the Mojave? I trained down there with the army once. Are you sure you know what you're doing?"

When I began to climb up westward out of Needles I was not quite sure what to expect, beyond a different sample of America. I knew there would be few relics of the old frontier: frontiersmen had steered clear of the Mojave. And the map and what little I had glimpsed as we dashed south in darkness suggested a different kind of desert from the Colorado. There would be no deep valley with eroded tentacles groping down into it. Instead, I would find a succession of long, sweeping slopes. These slopes made the pattern of my 150-mile route clear and simple: a protracted climb to a high pass; then an equally gradual descent to the trough of Death Valley.

This part of it turned out much as I had expected; in four days and sixty miles out of Needles I climbed five thousand feet so gradually that I was rarely conscious of going uphill. But the Mojave was at first anything but a scorched and empty wilderness. It began by presenting some of its own special brand of people. Next it produced a north wind that cut through me as if I were a ghost. Then it staged an all-day extravaganza. Only on the long descent into Death Valley did it begin at last to live up to its reputation.

"Water?" said the old man.

He peered at me closely, squinting into the setting sun. An old-fashioned green eyeshade made him look humorously quaint, like a hick-town newspaper editor by Norman Rockwell out of Mark Twain; but the sunlight showed up without pity the lined pallor of his face and the crumpled grubbiness of his clothes.

"Sure I can spare some water," he said. "Thought maybe you'd be needing it when I saw you stop and camp out here in the open. Just bring your canteens over to my store."

I followed him across the road toward the tumbledown store that stood so alone and obviously abandoned in the flat desert. Five minutes earlier I had passed the padlocked front door and smiled at its crude sign: YES, WE'RE STILL OPEN!

The old man kept squeezing staccato remarks back at me, punctuating them with a suck-and-click sound almost as loud as the words. "Don't get many people out here these days . . . (suck-and-click) . . . Not since they put the new highway in . . . (suck-and-click) . . . No need for you to sleep out in the open, you know . . . Plenty room in those old autos . . ." He nodded past two rusty gasoline pumps at a graveyard of automobiles. "Plenty room on the backseats . . . Plenty room in the back . . ."

He turned through a garden gate. Two chained dogs let him pass. As I followed, they erupted toward me, barking furiously, eyes staring and frenzied. Their chains brought them up half a yard short. The old man walked on.

We went through a side door and it slammed behind us. After the sunlight, the place was almost pitch dark. All around pressed disturbing black shapes. The smell of cooking lay thick, like a film of grease.

"Give me your canteens and I'll fill 'em for you," said the old man, and left me among the shapes.

Out of the blackness came sounds of dipping and pouring. "Good fresh water, too . . . ," rasped the old man's voice. "Only had this can up here a month . . ." In the dark, the sucks and clicks seemed to take longer than the words. "What'll you do about cooking? I don't allow no fires around here . . . But I'll be finished with the stove inside of five minutes, and if you like you can cook in here."

"Well, thank you."

"Best go get your pots and food . . . Then you can get down to work right away . . . And you can move your gear into an auto too . . . Plenty room in the back . . ."

When I returned, the old man sat in an inner room, crouched beside an oil heater. Around the heater a square of cardboard boxes had been stacked up like a fortification. A bare light bulb cast a pool of light down into the square.

Beneath the eyeshade, the old man's face was stained a ghostly green. "Just having breakfast," he said. He stirred the contents of a saucepan that stood on the heater. "Started cooking at two o'clock, but only just gotten 'round to it . . . Still, food that cooks slow is best."

I moved into the pool of light.

"Didn't take you long out there . . . ," said the old man. "D'you find a good auto?"

"Well, actually," I said, "I thought I might as well stay out in the open."

The old man looked up sharply. Black eyes stared at me from green shadow. "You'd best move into one of the autos . . . Better protected . . . Plenty room in the back."

"Oh, I don't think it'll rain." The black eyes stayed fixed on mine. "I guess I'll stay out in the desert."

The eyes blinked, then dropped. The old man gave a few sucks and clicks on their own before he rasped, "Push that stuff aside and sit down."

I cleared away a layer of magazines and unearthed a bench.

The old man took his saucepan off the heater, rested it on his knees, and motioned me to put my pot in its place.

We sat in silence. Every two or three minutes my host took a spoonful of beans from his saucepan and chewed them with deep concentration, staring in front of him at my cooking pot.

Suddenly he looked at his watch, grunted, and switched on a radio. A ranting voice filled the room, selling Christianity as if it were soap.

The old man crouched beside the heater, listening intently and still staring at my pot.

At last the voice stopped. The old man switched off. "A fine man," he said. "A very fine man."

I got up and tested the water in my pot. It was barely tepid.

We sat on in silence. At last I asked the old man if he could sell me something to eat cold while I was waiting. He brought a can of baked beans, but refused to let me pay for it. "No," he said. "They're my contribution to the trip." For the first time, he smiled. Even in the green stain of the eyeshield, it was a kind smile.

He sat down beside the heater again and stared at my pot. Occasionally he took a spoonful from his saucepan. I ate my can of cold beans.

Soon another voice, cousin to the first, boomed out from the radio.

On the heater, my pot showed no sign of boiling.

After fifteen minutes the voice ceased. The old man switched off. "Another fine man . . . ," he said. "A worthy messenger of God. A very fine man indeed . . ."

We went back to silence and pot watching.

"There!" said the old man at last. "Boiling!"

We ate in silence.

It was only when I began to collect my things together that he started to talk. Then, suddenly, it was as if a dam had burst. The sucks and clicks were swept away before the flood.

"Guess you'll be gone when I get up in the morning," he began. "I wake up around eight, but I pray 'til nine. *Used* to pray at night, around one or two o'clock. But it used to wake him up. Shows you how sensitive a man can be. Yes, it used to wake him up . . ." The words rolled out in an unstoppable flow, so confused that I grasped only the broad outlines of his meaning. He made no distinction between people who were present and those apparently elsewhere. It seemed there was another man somewhere—he didn't say where—to whom he "talked."

". . . And then there was this woman in Sacramento. She had this attack and her heart stopped beating. I heard him say it—right in the middle of the night it was—I heard him say, 'she's gone! She's gone!' 'No she hasn't!' I said. And right away I got down to work and prayed. Inside of two seconds —it can't have been more than two long seconds —I heard her heart start again. Just shows you how sensitive a man can be."

He waved the saucepan at me. His eyeshade tilted and the bare light bulb painted a white triangle on one cheekbone. Black eyes stared at me from the green face.

I took a step toward the door. "Well . . . ," I began, trying not to sound uncomfortable.

"Then there was this friend of mine in Nevada that wrote and told me he was going to have an operation. So I got down to work and prayed. Next morning the doctor came in and said, 'You don't need an operation after all. We can fix you up without one.' So he was all right that time. But later on he had to have another operation. He didn't write and tell me about this one. If I'd known, maybe I could have saved him that time too."

I began to feel faint. The cold numbness wrapped itself around me like a mist. I gripped the edge of a cardboard box. It bent beneath my fingers.

Without taking his eyes off mine, the old man put down his saucepan. The white triangle reappeared on his cheekbone. It was blurred now, like headlights seen through a wet windshield.

And suddenly I sensed that he was willing the faintness on me. He wanted to keep me there—to demonstrate his "power" and at the same time to fend off his loneliness. Evil flowed out from the green face, the same evil I had felt pulsating out from the rattlesnakes.

"And then there was this woman in San Francisco . . ." The voice came from far away now. "She wasn't sick before, but . . ."

I dropped my spoon and bent quickly down.

The old man's voice stopped.

I could see the spoon glinting in a shaft of light; but I stayed with my head between my legs, pretending to look for it. Slowly the blood drained back.

"Can't you find it?" The voice sounded a little closer.

I muttered something indistinct and stayed bending down. Slowly the numbness lifted. At last I reached for the spoon and stood up.

The old man was still staring at me. But the flow of words had stopped. His eyes no longer shone.

I said good-bye hurriedly. Too hurriedly. I knew I was hurting him; but all I could think of was escape.

Outside, the air was cool, almost liquid. By the time I reached the foot of the garden, it had dispelled the last trace of faintness. The two dogs, snarling into my flashlight at the limit of taut chains, presented a solid, friendly menace.

In the last rays of the setting sun, the cluster of buildings that was Goffs did not look the sort of place to be unduly worried by automobiles. Or, for that matter, to be worried by anything very much.

Two dogs greeted me. They streaked out from the first building, barking with the frenzy that self-respect demands of every country dog before he has reconnoitered a stranger; then, convention satisfied, they licked hands. Neither was more than a puppy. The brown one with a hint of spaniel lay on his back and asked for his belly to be scratched. The Heinz terrier stood on his hind legs and laughed with joy at being so unwashed.

I went into the store from which the dogs had erupted.

A tall woman with flowing white hair stood behind the counter. She beamed at me through horn-rimmed glasses. "Come in, come in," she said. "I heard you were on your way. The school bus driver passed you back down the road this afternoon. She brings us all our news." I remembered the friendly, peering driver who had waved to me. It was easy to imagine how she brought the news, good and bad, from everywhere to Goffs.

Around a table sat three men. Two of them were very old, the third about sixty. All three had that indefinable air of being about to eat.

"Do you serve meals?" I asked the woman with white hair.

"Well, we're only a store really . . ."

"Oh. Perhaps there's a cafe in town?"

The woman smiled. "I'm afraid not," she said. "There isn't much beyond here. In fact . . . well, you might say we *are* Goffs."

"I'll say you are," called the youngest man at the table. "Without Mrs. Craig there wouldn't *be* no Goffs." He waved a bottle of beer at her in salutation and homage. His flushed face was round and cheerful.

Mrs. Craig waved a bottle back in mock protest. "You watch your step, Jim Taylor," she said. "You watch your step." She turned back to me. "Guess you're feeling pretty hungry. How far have you come?"

A man appeared at a side door. He stood there unsteadily, trying to focus on my pack. "Whatchyer doing in *thish* part o' the country?" he asked aggressively. "We don' wan' none o' your . . ."

"That's enough, Tom," said Mrs. Craig. "Looks like the fresh air hasn't done you much good after all. Pull yourself together and lay the table—for six. This young man doesn't know it yet, but I'm asking him to supper. Come on now, Tom."

"Well," I said, "that's certainly very . . ."

"Of *course* you're staying. Take that great pack off your back and sit down with the rest of us. This is a birthday party."

The man for whom fresh air had failed to do much good still stood in the doorway. "We don' wan' none o' your promotion deals here," he said. "We've had too many proshpectors coming in with phony . . ."

"Stop that, Tom Craig," said Mrs. Craig. "Stop it right now. This young man's our guest, and I won't have you behaving that way. You go get the dishes right away . . . right away." The man retreated.

The birthday party was for Tom Craig's father. "Eighty-seven and sprightly as ever," said Mrs. Craig. The only other guests were a friend of the same vintage and Jim Taylor, the man who thought Mrs. Craig *was* Goffs.

When the party broke up about midnight, Jim

Taylor insisted I sleep in his trailer. "Can't have you sleeping outside when there's a spare bed in Goffs." As I followed him over to the trailer in bright moonlight, I saw that he moved his big body awkwardly, as if in pain.

I rolled out my sleeping bag on a bunk near the door. Jim sat on a bunk at the far end.

"You know," he said, "I don't like this idea of you walking across that desert alone. If I was half the man I used to be, I'd put you in the car tomorrow and take you up beyond Lanfair. You'd have to wrassle with me before you walked . . . Yessir, you'd have to wrassle with me . . . Here, take a nip of this bourbon.

"But I can't do it no more. Guess you could say I was living on borrowed time. Broke my neck twice these last few years. First time in an auto accident. Second time, a car knocked me down. Last July that was . . . Here, have another nip."

He climbed into his bunk.

"Yessir, you'd have to wrassle with me . . . Not that I ever did nobody any harm. I raised two boys—and they was both killed in World War II. I went through the first war myself. But I wasn't killed. Maybe better if I had been, 'stead of raising two kids to be killed in the second one . . . And I never did nobody any harm." There was no complaint in his voice. Just surprise that the world had not treated him better.

"You know, I spent most of my life in cities. In the city they'll knife you for a nickel. But it's not like that out here in the desert. Take the way I live in Goffs now. A friend o' mine gives me this trailer for free. And the Craigs won't charge me a cent for parking. Don't know what I'd do without them. Mrs.

Craig, she's a gem, like you saw. And old Tom, he's a good guy when he's sober. No sir, you won't find another Goffs in a hurry . . . not another place like Goffs, not even in the desert." His voice tailed away.

Moonlight streamed through a window onto the empty bourbon bottle.

Through the open door floated thin, eerie, attenuated music. It sang in quarter tones, like a Hindu chant; but the rhythm was less subtle, more Western. The volume increased. Moment by moment, rhythm gained dominance over melody. In a final, shattering climax, percussion prevailed. The train crashed past. The trailer trembled. By degrees, the noise subsided. But long before the uneasy rails were singing their Hindu chant again, the trailer was reverberating to a different rhythm.

Jim Taylor was thunderously asleep.

Next morning I went to say good-bye to the Craigs. On the way, the school bus passed. The driver—she who brought the news to Goffs—waved to me, as to an old friend.

Mrs. Craig spoke distractedly. Behind her glasses, she seemed on the verge of tears. "I'm sorry, but I'm not myself this morning," she said. "We've just had bad news. We've been looking after two young dogs for a friend of ours who's in the hospital. Concussion from an automobile accident. He wouldn't have sold those dogs for a million dollars, not for a million dollars. Every night, my Tom locked them up. But last night—'cause of the party I guess—he didn't shut their door properly. The driver of the school bus has just been in, and she says they've both been run over—by the same car it looks like—down the road a little ways. Stone dead, both of them. Stone dead."

All at once I remembered how Goffs had greeted me. "The dogs," I said. "Not a little brown one and a sort of wire-haired terrier?"

"That's right," said Mrs. Craig. "The friendliest little things in the world, they were . . . the friendliest little things in the world."

I woke up, and raised my head above the cattle trough. The wind hit me like a sheet of ice. I lowered my head.

There at four thousand feet, the rising sun kindled no warmth. For an hour I lay cocooned in my mummy bag, assuring myself that fifteen miles to the next water was an easy walk on such a day. Four inches above my nose, a metal flap on the end of the trough rattled and moaned. Flecks of ice clung to the stonework around it. Somewhere out in the scrub, a bird complained against the wind and the flatness of the country.

When the sun had melted the ice and made the world habitable again, I got up. After breakfast I walked on westward along the dirt road that cut like an arrow across the plateau.

Slowly the sun gained strength. But all day the wind remained in command.

It struck discords from the forest of Joshua trees that stretched back, mile after mile, like a huge decaying orchard. It scythed across the carpet of flowers and set them all shivering. It faced a group of cattle downwind and set their coats on edge. It moaned through the eye sockets of a whitened steer's skull. It whistled through the walls of a stone shack that stood roofless and rejected, miles from nowhere. And when stray clouds hid the sun it probed my marrow.

In mid-afternoon the sun made walking pleasant. But at every halt the wind renewed its edge.

I climbed higher toward a five-thousand-foot pass. The sun sank lower. The wind mounted. It funneled down from gray peaks and whipped across the sandy road. It mutilated my brief conversation with the only person I saw all day—a friendly Game Warden driving home from a trip into the hills.

The wind grew bitter with the promise of night. I found it difficult to believe that this was the Mojave Desert, and that I was pushing ahead at a steady fifteen miles a day because of the heat of Death Valley.

I climbed up into the pass. Stunted junipers replaced the Joshua trees. The wind increased.

I found the wind pump I was looking for and camped under the lee of a ruined cabin. It was one of four empty shells on the site of what had in Indian days been a government fort, and from its crevices the wind re-created a choir of ghostly war cries. They let me fall asleep at last; but an hour later I woke and for the first time since Mexico put on warm clothes in bed.

The night honed the wind's edge; but by next afternoon the sun had almost gained parity.

That afternoon I detoured along a granite escarpment. There is something strong and simple and honest about granite country. It has its surprises too. Without warning I would walk into a secret hollow. Brown granite walls held the wind at bay and reflected the sun's heat. Gleaming crystals paved the floor. At the far end, stone stools for high priests ringed a sacrificial altar. Before it, two gnarled junipers prostrated themselves. And cacti decorated every little shrine.

That night I slept in a sheltered granite cleft. The rock had basked all afternoon in the sun, and long after dark it was still warm to the touch. But the escarpment was higher than the old government fort, and I wore thick clothing to bed. An hour later I woke sweating—and understanding why rock cracks are favorite homes for cold-blooded rattlesnakes.

At sunrise I huddled in a niche on the edge of the escarpment and photographed a broad depression I had to cross. A thousand feet below, a drab green plain sloped gently away to the left. Thirty miles away, it leveled off in a natural sink that had gathered, as a sink drain gathers scum, a wasteland of sand dunes. The first sunlight set the dunes burning with their daily heat; but beyond, on mountains that folded back to impossible distances, snowcaps glistened. And up on my escarpment, as soon as I stepped out into the wind, my wrists were anesthetized.

I started down the escarpment. With every step, the wind's edge grew blunter. The junipers thinned out, vanished.

I reached the plain.

It was no longer drab green, but streaked with yellow and purples and reds. And the flowers no longer shivered; they danced in a gentle breeze that on its way had touched a furnace and been tamed.

By midday it was hot. I halted in a sheltered wash. After lunch I stretched out on the soft sand and gloried in the sun. Sweat trickled down my face.

The flesh lives strictly in the present. There in the

wash, the vicious north wind had already faded into a past of doubtful reality. But now the present all too clearly foreshadowed the future. Death Valley was suddenly very real indeed.

I crossed the trough of the depression, leaving the sand dunes far off to the left, and camped at Marl Spring. At sunrise next morning I started westward up an old trail.

Seventeen miles ahead was my first buried water. At least, I hoped so. On the drive south, after making caches in Death Valley, I had discovered a waterless thirty-odd miles between Marl Spring and the little settlement of Baker. In a sandy wash halfway between I had buried a five-gallon bottle of water. On the bottle I had put a note:

> If you find this cache, please leave it. I am passing through *on foot* in April or May, and am depending on it.

I had camouflaged the site carefully and marked it with a big black stone.

As I walked up the trail from Marl Spring I kept telling myself I would have no difficulty in finding that stone. If memory failed, I had a sketch map. Nothing could go wrong . . . unless somebody had seen the disturbed sand before the March rains had smoothed it; unless the rains had created a new watercourse and swept everything away; unless wind or water had piled a sandbank over the cache; unless . . .

I lengthened my stride.

The trail reached the far lip of the depression, hesitated, then dipped downward. A new view opened up. The nearer slopes were broken by black lava hills. But beyond them an immense openness sank down and away into the distance until it flowed at last into the foot of a huge, hazy mass. Somewhere through those mountains cut the trough of Death Valley. I stood four thousand feet above sea level; and the newly risen sun was already hot on my bare legs. Death Valley sank nearly three hundred feet below sea level. And the sun was getting hotter every day.

Soon the trail petered out. But a wash led directly down to my water cache, and I strode on over firm sand. Only sixteen miles to go. All I had to do was forget my cameras for once and concentrate on getting to the cache.

But the Mojave chose that day to stage its extravaganza. Scene after provocative scene cajoled, beckoned, tempted, titillated, and generally did its best to seduce the photographer in me.

It began with the usual Carmen come-on of flowers. Red Indian paintbrushes lit my way like torches. A fragile mauve brandy glass, translucent and exquisitely veined, delighted me with the shock of its five scarlet-feather inlays.

Carmen was naturally escorted by soldiers. A squad of six yucca cacti stood back to back, isolated but defiant, green bayonets thrust fiercely out in defense of six glorious white blooms. "Women in the center!" the yuccas seemed to cry (sweeping Carmen Jones into the Wild West), "and don't shoot 'til you see the whites of those damned Indians' eyes." Beyond the yuccas, a detachment of prickly cactus puppets defended a volcanic boulder. Each fat little soldier leaned outward from the defensive ring and gesticulated with stubby puppet arms. But they all seemed to be keeping an eye on the easy line of retreat that ran down right center stage.

The backdrop was extravagant too. Black conical hills crowded close. Tongues of lava licked the edges of the wash. Distant snowcaps floated above sand dunes and a dazzling soda lake.

And every stage property played its part. Wiry bush parasites built miniature orange igloos. Leopard-spotted lizards fled on sight. Their dazzle-painted cousins cocked heads on one side and quizzed the camera.

No man with warm photographic blood in his veins could be expected to withstand such well-staged witchery. I was quickly seduced. And the lovemaking proved so diverting that in three hours I covered rather less than three miles.

People who aim no higher than embalmed studies of Aunt Fanny outside the drugstore never seem to understand how photography eats up time. If one of them had come with me that morning he might have seen glimmerings of light. It was not just that exasperation and loving care had to fight their usual battles, first against each other, then as allies against form balance, shadows, depth of focus, light fluctuations, parallax, and a wobbly tripod. I also had to cope with the flimsy temperament of lizards, with the irresistible beckonings of a yet more brilliant display every time I moved forward for a flower shot, and with a fifty-pound pack that had to come off for almost every shot and then go back on again. After three hours of it, even a box-camera beginner would have grasped how it can take you three hours to go three miles.

At nine o'clock I solemnly swore to photograph for no more than ten minutes in each hour. Then I stalked on down the wash.

But the Mojave's extravaganza went on, hour after hour. Sometimes the scenes were miniatures. At the eleven o'clock halt I watched a fly transporting past my toes a green caterpillar six or seven times its own size. The fly had short wings and long legs. For walking, it used only one of its many pairs of legs; the remainder it wrapped around the caterpillar. With its burden underslung like a bomb, it struggled for yards across uneven sand, buzzing its wings when in difficulty. At last it dropped the caterpillar beside a small hole and disappeared head first. Its head reappeared. A pair of long legs reached out and dragged the caterpillar out of sight. My watch said the performance—and the halt—had run on for twenty minutes.

About lunchtime the weather began to back up the Mojave's bid to delay me. Thin clouds drifted down from the north. They circled and coalesced. The breeze died. The overcast thickened, and humidity magnified the heat. The sand grew softer. I plodded on, telling myself again and again that this was not going to be one of those days on which the will to walk just seeps away. At a mid-afternoon halt I leaned against my pack—and woke up fifteen minutes later. At teatime, while I was wondering how two furry black caterpillars managed to cross the glowing embers of my fire without turning a hair, I fell asleep again.

And so it went on as I trudged down the slope of a stage that was as rich in sideshows as a circus—and as unlike the Mojave of evil reputation as the windswept plateau had been.

Afternoon eased into evening. The sand grew progressively softer. I forced up my pace—and kept finding it had slackened again. At last, about six o'clock, I came to a familiar lava flow. Six weeks earlier I had parked the car beside it and carried a huge bottle of water over the lava flow, down a gully on the far side, and into a sandy wash.

Now, the trail on which the car had stood no longer existed. Heavy rains had scoured deep into the gravel. If rain had also scoured the wash on the far side . . .

I climbed up onto the lava flow. Six weeks earlier it had been a gloomy, brooding place. Now, even in fading light, it blazed with flowers. I walked across the lava through air heavy with perfume. I reached the edge of the lava. At my feet ran the gully. I peered down. The sand had not been scoured or built up; and beside a bush lay the black marker stone. I was almost sure it had not been moved. Tiredness gone, I bounced down the gully.

Then I stopped dead.

I heard myself say "Oh!" The extravaganza had kept for its finale the most breathtaking spectacle of all. At the foot of the gully, two ethereal yellow orbs floated above the sand. Their petals glowed with a luminous magic.

As I reached for my camera it occurred to me that no sane man who had walked across three hundred miles of flower-filled desert, who had been crushing flowers underfoot all day long, who was tired and hungry and still not certain his cache was intact, no sane man would . . . I opened the camera.

By the time I had taken one photograph the light had lost its luminosity and the two yellow visions their ethereal glow. They had become flowers. Very beautiful still, but mere earthbound flowers.

Sad that the curtain had fallen at last, I went over to the bush, moved the stone, and dug out the huge bottle. The water was clear as the day I buried it. The note was smudged by rain but still legible.

I drank a cupful of the cool water, then walked out into the wash to look for a better campsite.

As I walked, the gray desert began to grow lighter. I stopped and looked up. Directly overhead, an arc of sunlight streamed out of a break in the clouds and plunged like a flamethrower onto a range of black lava hills.

But the lava hills were no longer black. They were not even fiery red. They had passed beyond mere heat, beyond incandescence, to something purer. They glowed with a radiant magenta that was never one single and definable color but bloomed and swelled and expanded into a thousand transplendent hues until the whole line of hills was a pulsating mosaic held fast between black lava and gray sky.

The end was a slow diminishing. Finally, a time came when the purple of infinite royalty was no longer purple but black.

And standing there in the gray wash, a little breathless, with the wind blowing suddenly cold in my face, I knew that in the extravaganza's finale I had at last seen the climax the desert had withheld that evening beside the Colorado when I looked out beyond the tules and watched the Arizona hills catch fire. Now, remembering the pulsations that had just died, I understood for the first time something of the magic that binds people to the desert; and I seemed to hear as well not only another of the hints the jumping fish had given—those hints of a real reason for The Walk—but also a final assurance that I need not try to force the secret. In fact, that I *must* not try. If I left the reasons to look after themselves it would all be clear in the end.

I walked slowly back to the water cache and went to sleep among the flowers.

Next day, as I walked toward the little settlement of Baker, I began at last to see how the Mojave came by its reputation.

I was cutting for about 150 miles across a relatively high corner of the Mojave's fifteen thousand square miles. And this was only April; summer had hardly begun to stoke up. Yet, although Baker stood a thousand feet above sea level, the desert had already become truly desert-like. Most of the flowers had shriveled away. Even the creosote bushes looked weak and ailing. And, for the first time since my shortcut through the Colorado side canyons, I began to notice the heat.

Baker was a populated road junction of the gasoline age. A thermometer at the first gas station registered 91 degrees.

"This afternoon it hit ninety-four," a bouncy little man assured me. "Yessir, it'll soon start warming up."

He ran beady eyes over my pack. "What's that? Going through Death Valley? Huh, your feet must be stronger than your head. It'll be a hundred and ten up there by now. And climbing every day. I spent years right in the Valley, all summer too, so I know. I'm a real Desert Rat, I can tell you, a real Desert Rat."

"What sort of temperatures do they get on the floor of the Valley?" I asked—and waited.

If you are going to travel in strange country you must command a certain proficiency in the art of sifting fact from embroidery. The only reliable informant is the man who both knows what he is talking about and is not afraid to admit he doesn't know everything. You don't meet such men every day. The surest way of finding out if you have met one is to ask questions to which you know the answers.

I knew the Death Valley temperature position accurately. All-time high is a questionable 134 degrees, set in 1913, that for many years held the world record. Later and more dependable readings have never risen above 127 degrees. Most years, the limit is 124 or 125 degrees.

The Baker Rat pounced on my bait. "Summer temperatures in the Valley?" he said. "Well, I can't quote exact figures, but it gets hot, believe me. Here in Baker we have summer highs of a hundred and twenty-five or thirty. And sometimes . . ."—he turned to his wife—". . . sometimes we run to a hundred thirty-five, don't we?"

"Oh, not very often, dear."

"No, not too often. But it happens. And you can add a good twenty degrees for the Valley. So you'd best get ready to sweat a bit, my lad."

Beyond Baker, the Mojave plain sank steadily away for fifty miles toward the mountains that concealed Death Valley. Mile by mile, the desert grew barer. The flowers vanished. The vegetation became sparser, the soil sandier. Day by day, the heat festered toward a head.

So as to be fresh for Death Valley, I planned to rest for a day at Saratoga Spring at its south end. And I decided to use the fifty miles of road between Baker and Saratoga Spring as insurance in a safe trial run for the Valley itself. Each morning I was on the move before sunrise. By nine or ten o'clock the day's ten-mile stint was over. A wind that originated in hell might touch off a wrestling match with my poncho, but eventually I would get it stretched out between creosote bushes and crawl thankfully into its shade.

And there I would lie most of the day, reading a book or worring about minor physical details of the sort that in normal life hardly rate higher than the color of your toothbrush. These things had all along loomed large in my thoughts. (Later, I was astonished to find *how* large. My notes included reams of ponderous information on such matters as the position and convalescent state of my only blister and the exact limits of brown-as-a-berryness on my body.)

Those last hot days before Death Valley, the little details ruled my world.

Just before Baker I had begun an experiment as momentous to me as the launching of a new model to General Motors: I tried walking without a shirt. Would the pack straps rub? Would dehydration be excessive? Would I sunburn? Would I really feel fresher? A week of lengthening trials produced a definite no to the first three questions and a resounding yes to the fourth. (It also produced a homely little note that one shoulder burned browner than the other.)

But the day I left Baker, cramp-like pains began to attack my legs and shoulders. By evening I felt a little light-headed. I plodded along the road meditating on the drama of catching polio in Death Valley, and extracting an obscure pleasure from it. But soon I remembered a conversation with a Death Valley Ranger on the way south.

"By mid-April, when you get this far," he had said, "it'll be warming up, and you'll likely find you need extra salt. I only take one tablet a day myself. My stomach won't accept more. But one man here takes twenty. If he doesn't, he ends up in the hospital with heat exhaustion. So you'll have to figure out for yourself how many you need."

The evening beyond Baker I took two tablets. The pains eased. Next day I sucked a tablet every hour I walked. By the fourth day I was taking an eight-tablet dose, and the pains had vanished. With them went the last vestiges of faintly pleasurable worry. There are times when, like all hypochondriacs with any charity, I feel sorry for those who endure minor ailments with stoicism. They miss so much.

The salt deficiency was remedied only just in time. On the fourth morning beyond Baker, almost at the foothills of the mountains, I cut away from the road; and at six o'clock I crossed the unmarked boundary of Death Valley National Monument.

The sun had been up for barely an hour, but already the plain felt like a hot plate. Just beyond the Monument border, the last stunted shrubs thinned into extinction. I trudged on over bare gravel toward Saratoga Spring. Only four miles to go now, and then a day's rest.

Soon the salt flats began. At first the crust was firm

and dry. Then my feet began to break through and to slip and slither on the wet undersurface. The sun beat down from glaring blue sky; its reflection beat up from glaring white salt. Sweat dripped down my bare back. Once, I stopped to take a photograph. The act demanded considerable concentration. Afterward, heaving up the pack was a major effort. I plodded on again through glaring whiteness. The heat hammered at me from every side, pounding my brain into a hard, impervious disk.

At last, out near the tip of a foothill ridge, I saw something green. Slipping and slithering on the wet salt, I struggled toward it.

Warm water lapped deliciously around my shoulders and caressed my naked body.

I stood on tiptoe and looked out through a gap in the tules that fringed the pool. Six feet away began the salt flats that I had been struggling across ten minutes earlier. Their whiteness palpitated in the heat.

I looked down through the clear blue water. All around my feet, miniature springs were flinging up little brown puffballs of sand. I swam slowly across the pool and tiny fish scattered before me. Some were silvery, some a brilliant aquamarine. I climbed out and stood in the sun until I was dry. Then I went back into the shade of a huge tamarisk tree.

All morning I sprawled there, naked and cool, feeling like Adam in the Garden of Eden.

At lunchtime I was collecting firewood from a pile of old lumber when I became conscious of a faint buzzing, like a fly on a windowpane. A wind was rustling the tamarisk tree, and I bent down to listen more closely to the buzzing sound. Then I stepped quickly back. Beside the lumber lay a rusty ax. I picked it up and pushed aside a plank. The buzzing increased. Then I saw, close to where my hand had been, a thin, mottled body. It began to wriggle into a hole between two stones. Before the snake disappeared—still rattling faintly—I got in a jab with the ax. Afterward, there was blood on the stone.

I was back under the tree that grew in my Garden of Eden before I realized that the serpent had not emitted evil. This time, like Eve, I had felt only curiosity.

I lolled away the afternoon in the shade of my tamarisk tree. Among its branches flickered sleek birds that in shadow were jet black but in sunlight exploded into iridescent blue. At rare intervals they breathed out a soothing melody, so "liquid" that I might have been lying beside a mountain brook. The day's only imperfections were huge black flies that bit with malice and precision. Fly dope was quite useless against them. After scoring direct hits I fed the corpses to a tiger-barred lizard who sat on a water canteen and accepted them on the end of a stick, like cocktail cherries.

In my two days at Saratoga Spring there were only two interruptions. A man who had been rock hunting from his pickup truck in nearby canyons, basing himself on the spring, came back briefly. He was, he said, pulling out because of the heat. That morning, up on the hill, he had felt "real dizzy." He gave me a gallon bottle of fresh water that he had "found under a pile of stones, back up in the hills." It tasted far better than the alkaline spring water, but every time I took a drink I found myself wondering whether someone with this rock hound's free-and-easy attitude had stumbled on my own precious caches.

Soon after the rock hound left, two Death Valley Rangers came to check that I had arrived safely. (I had telephoned the Chief Ranger from Baker, as he had asked.) The rangers reported that the day before the temperature had touched 105 degrees. Minimum had been 80 degrees. When they drove away they took my sleeping bag. It weighed almost six pounds, and with night temperatures never dropping below 80 degrees I was hardly likely to feel cold.

On the drive south, I had studied the Valley's temperature records at Monument Headquarters. Cycles followed a well-defined pattern. Hot spells always built up slowly. Day after day the temperature rose steadily; then, overnight, it came plunging down. Comparative coolness lasted for a day or two; then the mercury began to creep up again. There seemed no reason to expect a sudden plunge now, and the more I thought about it the more thankful I felt that on the way south the Chief Ranger had persuaded me to bury my water caches only ten miles apart. Even so, the crucial fifty miles ahead promised five uncomfortable days.

In those fifty miles I would find no drinkable water except that in my buried caches. And Gravel Well, the first "natural" water, offered no shade; but Bennett's Well, a few miles beyond, was surrounded by mesquite bushes. For five days those mesquite bushes would be my target. Above Bennett's Well, more than eleven thousand feet up on the western wall of the Valley, towered the snowcap of Telescope Peak. For five days, the snow would be my beacon.

Meantime, I meant to spend my day's rest wallowing in the luxuries of Saratoga Spring.

The tamarisk tree and the aquamarine pool were not the whole oasis. Near the tree stood a small lath-and-plaster building. The rangers had said it was built years before as part of an unsuccessful attempt to commercialize the "medicinal" spring water. The swimming pool drained into a marsh with a shallow lake at its far end. That night, the marsh grew thunderous with frogs. And in the morning the lake supported an assembly of ducks that bickered like statesmen.

In mid-morning I climbed with my cameras into the hills behind the spring. Rock strata cut across their slopes in startling strokes of brown and black and red. A strong west wind was blowing, but the heat had lost none of its ferocity. The wind whisked the lake into a sparkling blue disk; beyond it, to the north, the salt flats still palpitated. To the left, two vertical miles above, hung the snow of Telescope Peak. To the right reared the escarpment of the Amargosa Range. And held fast between the two, like a corpse in its desert grave, stretched the gray trough that was Death Valley.

The wind increased. I climbed to the crest of a ridge. The wind rose to a half gale. In a careless moment, after using my hat to shield a camera lens, I forgot to slip the band back under my chin. Before I could lift a hand, the wind had snatched the hat away and sent it soaring upward like a hawk.

Suddenly the sun was battering down on my head like a bludgeon.

I cannot have stood there looking at the flying hat for more than two or three seconds. But I do not think I shall ever forget the feeling of helplessness as the twirling brown shape grew smaller and smaller. I stood still, watching it twist up and away into the hard blue sky.

The hat dived behind one of the fantastically colored ridges that stretched back and back as far as I could see. Its disappearance snapped the spell. I broke into a run. As I ran, I remembered Chickenhouse Smith looking at the magazine picture of a corpse sprawled beside its bicycle. "No hat—not surprised," he had said. I raced on over bare rock. A makeshift hat in Death Valley? I might go days without seeing anyone. And I could hunt for hours among those endless ridges without finding the hat. I scrambled onto a chocolate-brown crest. And there, its band neatly looped over a spike of rock, lay the hat.

Slowly I walked back down the hill. Now the danger had passed, I felt thankful that the desert had reminded me in time how fine a line divides safety from tragedy—and how easily a moment of carelessness can send you stumbling across it.

Back at camp, the tamarisk tree moaned in the wind. When I tried to write a letter, the paper tore in my hand. By four o'clock a full gale was blowing. The heat remained stifling.

Thirty miles to the west, a great wedge of sand funneled out from a gap in the mountains. It spilled down over the salt flats and obscured the sun. Up in the Valley, the heat haze thickened to a salt-and-sand haze.

The wind rose to a new pitch. It whipped the placid swimming pool into a debris-strewn frenzy.

Flying salt and sand stung my body. Above me, the tamarisk tree swayed and groaned. I kept looking at two fractures where heavy branches had recently snapped.

About six o'clock I moved into the little lath-and-plaster building.

Inside, the gale was no more than a gusty wind. Through the window I could see only a wedge of gray, sand-filled sky. I tried to read, but my thoughts kept straying to the crucial five days ahead. If the wind kept up, should I head north in the morning? With a sandstorm howling across the Valley, I might miss the water caches . . .

When the light failed I closed my book and leaned back against the wall. It shook beneath the buffeting of the wind. I sat and wondered if the cracks on the far wall were really growing wider.

CHAPTER

4

THROUGH DEATH VALLEY

I woke before dawn to the sound of tules rustling in a gentle breeze. The tamarisk tree was almost silent, the sky black and star filled.

At five o'clock, as day and landscape began to unfold, I crunched out over the salt flats. Out in the open, the breeze was a cool north wind. The sun rose without real warmth. It dug shadows in the pockmarked salt, then drained them away until a pure white coldness surrounded me. Far ahead, Telescope Peak answered the whiteness. Across the salt flats, I trod carefully to control wasteful slipping of my feet. On the far side there was a dirt road. I turned north along it.

It was at the first halt, as I sheltered from the wind behind a roadside bush, that the significance of the weather clicked into focus. And the new picture swept aside at a single stroke my whole carefully thought-out five-day plan.

At this time two days earlier I had been struggling across the salt toward Saratoga Spring. Sweat was dripping down my naked back; the heat was hammering from every side, pounding my brain into a disk. Now I was shivering behind a bush. And suddenly I saw that the gale had sent temperatures plunging into one of the recurrent Death Valley slumps. Almost before I remembered how soon the mercury would climb back over one hundred, I knew what I had to do.

By ten o'clock I had dug out the first water cache. Telescope looked little closer; but the sun was no more than warm. I ate lunch, then rested. At noon I undressed, and in the privacy of total openness poured all the spare water over myself. And at 12:30 I started northward again.

The afternoon was almost disappointingly normal. The heat passed its peak without anger. Telescope Peak eased closer. Two private cars and a heavy truck swept dustily past. When I reached the second water cache, an hour before sunset, I felt almost cheated. The double-header had been too easy. After twenty-one miles of the crucial fifty I felt less tired than at the end of many other desert days. All I needed was a good night's rest. After supper I put on my warmest clothing, curled up in a gully with the poncho wrapped around me, and fell asleep.

I suppose I should have known that the desert would come up with something new.

Before long, I came half awake and tried to pull the poncho closer around me. There was no wind—nothing that could even be called a breeze. But cool night air was moving slowly and steadily across the desert's surface. Like the tide advancing across mudflats, it penetrated every corner. It passed over me. It passed around me. It passed underneath me. Soon it seemed to be passing through me as well. Minute by minute it sucked away the warmth usually conserved so efficiently by my sleeping bag. No matter how close I cuddled to the gully wall, the cold bit deeper and deeper.

For shapeless hours I fought the sleep battle. Occasionally I dozed. More often I lay three-quarters awake, telling myself I was half asleep. By two o'clock the dozes had become unreal memories. At 3:30 I headed north into the darkness.

I found myself walking in a curious and disturbing state of detachment. The paleness that was the road refused to stay in positive contact with my feet. All around hovered hints of immense open spaces and distant, unconvincing slopes. Time had lost real meaning back in the gully; now it lacked even boundaries. My watch registered an hour and a half of black, detached nothingness. Then a paleness rimmed the eastern horizon and gave the landscape tenuous reality. Gray light revealed gray-brown stones, gray-blue slopes, gray-white snow on Telescope Peak.

I walked on with unrhythmic steps. The air movement became a northerly breeze. The sun rose behind a wind-wracked fan of cloud and hung there like a congealed egg. The breeze became a north wind. The map said 150 feet below sea level. I put on more clothes.

Two hours of frigid daylight and bemused walking, and I was digging out the third water cache. Telescope Peak, high above, looked suddenly close. Of the fifty crucial miles, thirty-three were past; in a little over twenty-four hours I had completed a three-day stint. It didn't seem to mean much.

I curled up in the lee of a sandy hummock and fell asleep.

Two hours later I was awake. The sun felt almost

hot. I rigged the poncho as an awning and crawled into its grave-size patch of shade. And all day I lay in the narrow parallelogram, moving over with the sun, striving to sleep and remaining obstinately awake. Occasionally I propped myself up on an elbow and studied Telescope Peak. It was so close that I could see, well below the snowcap, streaks of white clinging to what seemed impossible rock slopes. Only twelve miles to Gravel Well; only eighteen to Bennett's Well and the mesquite bushes that were my target. I still knew what I had to do.

At sunset I unrigged the poncho and wrapped it around me and at last drifted off to sleep. The slow air movement had already begun.

The cold did its work efficiently. By 9:30 I was on the move.

This time, bright moonlight made the night something real and conquerable. The snows of Telescope, white and pure, urged me on. The road was real too: something I could plant my feet on firmly and confidently. By eleven o'clock the mesquite bushes at Bennett's Well seemed almost within my grasp.

Then the moon set.

Telescope Peak vanished. Now, there were no scents or sounds. Just stillness and darkness and hints of colossal open space. The world narrowed to a blur that achieved reality only through jabbing at my feet. Distance degenerated into marks on the map. Time was the creeping progress of watch hands.

The night wore on, an endless belt of blur and blackness. Unreal walking. Halts. Restartings that took progressively more effort. Aching legs. Aching shoulders. Cold.

About one o'clock a shape loomed off to the right.

The map, dim beneath a failing flashlight, said "Salt Well" and "Tanks." A penciled note added "No drinking water, but good place for bath." I remembered scribbling the words back in San Francisco while a helpful Park Service man talked about the delights of a bath when desert sun had dried you out. Now, the sun was a year away. A century divided me from San Francisco.

There was only one interlude when I regained contact with reality.

It began with the pattering.

Was it in front or behind? It seemed to be first one, then the other. I laughed at myself: tiredness was no reason for being as fanciful as Moly in *The Wind in the Willows* when he went alone into the Wild Wood. But in unguarded moments I still seemed to hear the pattering.

The watch hands permitted a halt. I sat down and slipped off the pack. And then, close behind me in the darkness, something moved. I flicked on the flashlight. Four feet away, its big brown eyes looking directly into the beam, stood a fragile little fox-like creature. It showed no fear, only curiosity. It began to circle me, its bushy tail stretched stiffly out behind. It held its muzzle low, pretending to sniff the ground; but it kept darting sidelong glances, as a dog will when it wants to keep check on you but at the same time to appear immersed in important doggy business.

The flashlight grew dim and I switched off. The pattering circled me, very close. It had a trusting and friendly rhythm, more like that of a domestic animal than a wild one.

And then I thought of rabies. Rabid animals do not fear man. I remembered watching a rabid jackal wander across a harvested wheat field in Kenya. It had passed quite close, tossing its head and ignoring us completely. It had not been actively friendly like this, but . . .

I switched on the flashlight. The animal stood less than three feet away, sniffing at my staff. It was not tossing its head. No saliva flecked its jaws. It was looking at me appealingly, as if it wanted to be fed or stroked. But rabies . . . ! I made a "shooing" noise. The animal moved back. It seemed disappointed in me.

For ten minutes, as I sat in darkness, I heard little noises close by; and when I walked on, the pattering came with me—first on one side, then the other. I switched on the flashlight. The animal was trotting along beside me. It darted ahead, scampered across the road, and waited. When I came level it turned with a playful little pirouette and again trotted alongside. A kitten romping with a ball of wool could scarcely have had more fun. When I switched off the light I found I was listening to the pattering and smiling to myself in the darkness. The pack felt less heavy now, the night less blank, the road a little less stony.

After twenty minutes I realized the pattering had stopped. I switched on the flashlight. Nothing.

I trudged on into the lonely darkness.

Tiredness came flooding back. The stones jabbed up more fiercely. My pack was full of lead. Some of it had overflowed into my bloodstream, and one large ingot had lodged under the ball of my left foot. Only the cold prodded me on.

But at last, just after three o'clock, there was a road off to the left. A hundred yards, and my flashlight played weakly on the hand pump of Gravel Well. It was a struggle to make myself wash my feet before I wrapped the poncho around me, lay down on the nearest smooth ground, and instantly fell asleep.

I woke up at first light, numb as an iceberg. The "smooth" ground was a penance bed of pointed stones. Somebody was pounding with a hammer on the ball of my left foot. All I could think of was that it was only six miles to Bennett's Well and the mesquite bushes that were my target. And by eight o'clock, with the snows of my fifty-mile beacon at last hanging directly above, I was washing my feet under the pump at Bennett's Well.

It was fifty-one hours since I had crunched out from Saratoga Spring to face five days of heat. The ordeal that had been looming ever since Mexico was over almost before it had begun.

The act of driving your body, very occasionally, close to its limit of endurance is for some reason one of life's major satisfactions. And relaxing afterwards is one of life's most luxurious rewards.

I spent the day at Bennett's Well stretched out beneath a mesquite bush, dozing or gazing up at blue sky through a tracery of leaves. Gnats and bees buzzed lazy harmonies. From time to time a passing lizard paused to inspect me. Everything was warm and bright and unhurried.

But satisfied as I felt, I had to admit that the crucial fifty miles had in a sense been a disappointment. It had been right to make full use of the cool spell, but by rushing ahead I had lost sight of the objects of The Walk. Although I had gained an unexpected view of the desert, I had not really seen Death Valley—not even the one-third of its length I had walked through. But my route to Emigrant

Ranger Station kept to the Valley floor for another ten miles before it turned up a side canyon; and now I could afford to take a leisurely look.

There was only one uncertainty.

On the drive south I had called at Emigrant Station and discussed with Matt Ryan, the resident ranger, my plan to cut north over the crest of the Panamint Mountains. On the map, the route looked steep but feasible. Matt Ryan, trying hard to hide his disapproval of The Walk, had recommended a longer but less punishing route. The detour meant dropping back first onto the floor of Death Valley.

Matt Ryan was playing safe. In his place I should have done the same. He knew nothing about me, and as long as I stayed in his district he would be responsible for my safety, at least in his own mind. So I had not pressed for the direct route. Words were no good. But I felt fairly sure that if I walked into Emigrant Station in good shape and on schedule, Matt Ryan would believe I could look after myself.

Now, under the mesquite bushes at Bennett's Well, I decided to forget for the moment that I might have to come back down onto the floor of the Valley. I would just aim at reaching Emigrant Ranger Station on schedule. And that gave me six days to amble forty miles.

It looked at first as though sleep might remain a problem, but that afternoon a ranger brought out my sleeping bag. He was sure the little pattering animal that had followed me must have been a desert kit fox; they were often quite friendly. He also said that the maximum temperature had dropped from 105 degrees the day I rested at Saratoga Spring to only 80 degrees the next. The minimum fell from 80 to 58 degrees.*

With the mummy bag once more in my pack, I left Bennett's Well and walked on up the Valley. I took my time now, but at first I found myself failing to grasp the awesomeness of the scenery. The lack of appreciation may have been due in part to a sort of daze that came from sleeplessness and the aftermath of effort. But there was more to it than that.

The trouble with Death Valley as a spectacle is that its extremes are too extreme. It bombards you with the lowest land and the highest temperatures in America, with 282 feet below sea level and 11,049 above, with salt and snow, with mountains uncompromisingly mountainous and plains unbelievably plain. Everything is so big, so impossibly big, that your senses cannot really grasp the scale. Somehow, the landscape had lost its grandeur as soon as I moved up into the Valley from Saratoga Spring. Now, beyond Bennett's Well (perhaps because of the sheer scale of things, perhaps because of my sleepy daze, but more probably because of both) even time was affected.

---

*The 58 degrees surprised me. It had felt more like 38 degrees. Months later I realized that temperature readings are by no means the only factor affecting how cold you feel at night. Wind—even the slow desert air movement—can make all the difference. Official readings are taken five feet off the ground, shielded from air movement. But most important of all is plain getting used to cold. During the war I had often slept in snow, wrapped in a gas cape. But we were always doing it. By the time I reached Death Valley I had grown used to 90 or 100 degrees in daytime—and to a good warm mummy bag at night.

When I came to Tule Spring, my imagination quite failed to make the hundred-year flight demanded by its bronze plaque:

BENNETT'S LONG CAMP
NEAR THIS SPOT BENNETT-ARCANE CONTINGENT OF DEATH VALLEY FORTY-NINERS, EMIGRANTS FROM MIDDLE WEST, SEEKING SHORT CUT TO CALIFORNIA GOLD FIELDS, WERE STRANDED FOR MONTH AND ALMOST PERISHED FROM STARVATION. TWO YOUNG COMPANIONS, WILLIAM LEWIS MANLY AND JOHN ROGERS, MADE HEROIC JOURNEY ON FOOT TO SAN FERNANDO, RETURNING WITH SUPPLIES, AND LED PARTY TO THE SAFETY OF SAN FRANCISQUITO RANCHO NEAR NEWHALL.

Nor did the past jump to life as it should have done when I came to a pile of stones that the map simply called "grave." Its plaque said:

BURY ME BESIDE JIM DAYTON IN THE VALLEY WE LOVED. ABOVE ME WRITE: "HERE LIES SHORTY HARRIS, A SINGLE BLANKET JACKASS PROSPECTOR." EPITAPH REQUESTED BY SHORTY (FRANK) HARRIS, BELOVED GOLD HUNTER, 1856–1934.

HERE JAMES DAYTON, PIONEER,
PERISHED, 1898.

TO THESE TRAILMAKERS WHOSE COURAGE MATCHED THE DANGERS OF THE LAND, THIS BIT OF EARTH IS DEDICATED.

My first real grasp of time—and scenery—came when I made a two-mile pace-and-compass march across the salt flats to the lowest land in the Western Hemisphere. The lowest point was for many years taken to be Badwater, over on the east side of the Valley. It was a convenient arrangement. People could drive there on blacktop, lean out of car windows, touch a marker, and retail their experience for years. Then some tiresome surveyor discovered, far out on the salt flats, two adjacent points each 2.2 feet lower than Badwater. From the beginning I had for some reason made up my mind to visit one of them. Only three or four men were known to have made the pilgrimage.

By the time I reached the middle of the salt flats I understood the paucity of pilgrims. Nothing "marked the spot." On every side stretched a whiteness that looked level as a millpond. My feet sank three inches into wet salt.

But I stayed at the lowest point for an hour. There was nothing to see, I suppose, except white flatness and plunging blue mountains. But there was simplicity as well as starkness. And after a while I began to hear in the silence some whisper of the ticking aeons that had gone into making the salt and gravel layers that went down under my feet for a thousand feet and more. And I began to understand as well as to know that lakes had always come and gone on the floor of the Valley—a million years here, a million there—and that around their margins had prowled, at their evolving times, dinosaurs and mastodons and elephants. The vision had hardly materialized before it began to fade away. But when I retraced the straight line of my footprints back across the wet salt and then across caked mud and salt that creaked in the growing heat, I felt quietly glad that I had made the pilgrimage.

It was only when I climbed up a side canyon and walked out onto Aguereberry Point that I comprehended at last the magnificence of Death Valley.

For the first time I saw what I had walked through. Saw it, that is, as a coherent whole. The Valley floor, six thousand feet below and two days behind, was now far enough removed in both dimensions to have regained its mystery. Details had fused into a comprehensible pattern. Down the center ran the salt flats. Curving out into them from the mouth of every side canyon spread huge fans of gravel. Minor peaks stuck up from the gravel like icebergs, nine-tenths submerged. And the mountains—two massive walls facing each other across the trough—framed the pattern and held it together. The pattern itself was motionless. But across it flowed dark cloud-shadows, big as desert islands. It was seascape in reverse: racing islands hurling themselves across a static ocean.

Aguereberry Point turned out to be the right place to say good-bye to the Valley. It was one of those charmed places where everything goes right.

My elation started in a side canyon on the way up. First there was being back among flowers; after the barrenness of the Valley floor, it was like coming home. Then there was the inexplicable excitement of coming around a bend in the parched canyon and seeing, for the first time since Mexico, a snow-covered slope close enough for me to pick out individual trees. And when I climbed at last onto Aguereberry Point there was the urgent bite of mountain air.

I camped under an overhanging rock, with the Valley filling my picture window. It rained during the night, but an hour after dawn the last clouds swirled away across the reopening abyss. A rainbow arched out after them. Soon, sunshine once more filled the desert.

All day I sat and watched Death Valley. Nothing very much happened, I suppose. But snow had fallen overnight on nearby peaks, and again it kindled that odd excitement. All around, immense upended rock strata cut across the mountains in a pattern the mind could grasp. Clouds chased each other across the Valley floor. Colors changed. And once, as I stood on the brink of a precipice, two swallows plummeted past, inches apart, tearing the air. Holding position as if clamped together, they dipped over the precipice and swooped toward a sheer and jagged rock spire. Just as it seemed they would smash into its face, they surged up together in a great unexpected arc of freedom that carried them far out over the immensity of Death Valley and up at last to vanishing point in the blue desert sky.

I walked into Emigrant Ranger Station at sunset on May 1, dead on schedule.

Matt Ryan, the ranger, was sitting in the garden with his wife.

The first thing he said was, "How about a drink?"

The second, glass in hand, was, "You know, I've been thinking about your best route. The temperature down on the floor of the Valley is back over a hundred already. If you'd really like to, I don't see why you shouldn't go the way you wanted, directly over the Panamints . . ."

CHAPTER

5

BEYOND THE PANAMINTS

Nothing is more certain to make you appreciate a place than the knowledge you will soon be leaving it; and all through the final hundred miles of true desert I found myself seeing what went on around me as I had never done before. After two months the desert could still spring surprises, could still show me new faces. And now at last I had time to appreciate them.

I had been a little afraid that after the physical challenge of Death Valley I might suffer a sense of anti-climax. Instead, as soon as I climbed up into the Panamint Mountains I found new freedom.

Ever since Mexico, time had been tugging at my sleeve. Because of the Death Valley deadline, I had never been able to stand and stare without twinges of conscience. But now the pressure was off. Instead of always trying to get somewhere, I could give myself up to going.

So for two weeks I took my time, savoring both the desert's surprises and the details that had been there all along but which I had hardly noticed. At times I felt almost sorry for the man in my boots who for two months had scurried northward. I looked back at him as we always look back at ourselves—with smug wonder at the gulf between the innocent of yesterday and the sage of today.

The first day beyond Emigrant Ranger Station began as yet another physical challenge. Before sunrise I headed across a rough plain toward the forbidding eastern slope of the Panamint Mountains. As I crossed the succession of deep washes I remembered how on the drive south a young park assistant at Emigrant Station had opened his eyes wide when he learned which way I planned to go. "But you can't go up *there,*" he said. "That's *rugged*!"

Now the mountains reared up in front of me. The sun rose, and soon the whole range was baked brown and hard and lifeless. From the first five-thousand-foot crest tumbled tortuous ridges, sharp as knives. Canyons cut deep and cruel, like wounds.

But the threatened grimness never materialized. It melted away as usual among flowers and the sweep of immense distance. That night, after sliding and slipping two thousand feet down a talus slope on the far side of the crest, I camped among billowing trees. Through the trees tinkled a foot-wide creek, clear as crystal. It was the first running water I had seen since the Colorado.

I woke to bird song and the warmth of sunlight filtered through moving leaves. The play of light and shade was cool and liquid, like shadows rippling across the floor of a tropical lagoon. Against an opening of blue sky, birds and insects seemed to jostle for space; and among them drifted little puffs of thistledown, lifting and pirouetting in the breeze.

I sat up and leaned against a tree. Its massive trunk was ribbed and furrowed like an ancient sequoia in a rain forest. Its roots reached out into the life-giving creek. For six inches on either side of the water, plants grew rank and green, and the whole sandy canyon floor was a tangle of bushes and trees. Through a gap in them a slab of hot brown desert rock looked hopelessly out of place, like a flat from an old stage production left standing in the wings.

I lingered in camp almost all day watching the life that swarmed around the thin ribbon of water.

A huge brown moth glided down onto a weed bed and dipped its slender proboscis into the water; it drank, then curled the proboscis happily, like an elephant squirting sand, and flew away. A pair of dragonflies settled on a leaf and copulated; the brilliant azure male pinned the female's neck with his tail, and her brown body squirmed ecstatically. Two blue-bellied lizards necked on a stone. High above, a dove duet billed and cooed. Near my outstretched feet a dowdy brown sparrow pecked away at seeds and ignored her scarlet-spotted suitor, who gallantly drove off rivals and sang complicated serenades that always ended on the world's universal questing note.

Once, I heard a trumpeting that had become familiar along the final stretch of the Colorado. I pushed through to the edge of the trees. A hundred yards up the glaring slope stood the first wild burros I had actually seen. They eyed me curiously. Cream-colored muzzles and eye circles and under-markings stood out against their chocolate-brown coats. After a while the herd galloped off in a cloud of dust.

Two or three times I half-decided to move on; but the sun rose higher, and somehow I stayed. The scent of sun-warmed flowers permeated the canyon. Butterflies flickered past. Huge steel-blue flies with cigar-butt bodies planed about, seeming to do nothing for a living but drive away intruder cousins. Hummingbirds inspected me, uptailed and darted away, then returned for reinspection.

In late afternoon I struck camp at last and walked up beyond the creek's source spring. The canyon opened out into a broad and treeless valley, and I began to climb slowly up through rounded foothills. From a distance they were covered with a soft green nap.

In three days' easy walking through this pleasant land of the Panamints I saw no one.

The whole country rested beneath an almost tangible pall of silence and peace. It was obvious that man had not intruded since time began. And as usual the obvious was quite wrong.

The afternoon I left the creek, I followed a broad wash. Burro trails wound through it. But for them, I might have been walking on the face of the earth before life evolved into anything as complicated as us mammals. I was musing along these lines when I saw a dark object ahead. It had a straight, unnatural outline. Soon I was standing beside a metal post. From its head a finger pointed north and south, Ozymandias-like, over the lone and almost level sand:

←——————SURVEYORS WELL 20M
JACKASS SPRING 15M——————→

A metal tag warned:

DESTRUCTION OR INJURY OF
POST A STATE PRISON OFFENCE

The post was in perfect repair.*

Two days later, close to a permanent spring, I stumbled on a massive granite bowl embedded in the soil. The bowl was about eighteen inches long, a foot wide, and seven inches deep. Its sides and flat base were rough-hewn, but the shallow concave surface had been worked to a fine polish. Pressed into the earth under the bowl I found some charcoal and a few small fragments of bone. Nearby lay a long, roughly squared piece of granite with a small oval hole at one end.†

During those four days of solitude I stumbled on a few other signs of man: two feet of metal pipe turning a spring into a faucet; the shell of a cabin; the relics of what had once been a cattle corral.

---

*Months later, I discovered that a prospectors' route used to run through this valley. The wild burros were not necessarily these prospectors' strays, though. They could easily have moved in from a couple of hundred miles away. And so could the two small herds of wild horses, totaling about twenty head, that I stampeded that same day. There are few other places in California, outside the extreme north, that you can still find wild horses.

†Later, I discovered that these were an Indian mortar and pestle, used for grinding piñon and other wild seeds, especially grass. They probably belonged to Shoshone Indians, who would have used them right up to the time the white man came.

But their significance was lost beneath the peace and silence that lay over everything.

Then, on the fourth morning, I came to a road. It was only a narrow dirt road, hardly more than a track. But as I turned along it I felt sad. A road meant people—the first people since I walked away from Emigrant Ranger Station.

I need not have worried. For a week I followed the dirt road as it dipped down into a miniature Death Valley, then wound back up to within five hundred feet of the snow line. In that week I set eyes on about a dozen people. And all the time the desert kept showing me new faces.

Sometimes the faces were not really new: it was just that because the end of the desert was near I was seeing with new eyes what had been there ever since Mexico.

High in a rock crevice, a gleam of red. I scrambled up the steep gully. A cluster of prickly little brown shapes clung to the rock. And from their center, lifted to the sky like red-hot trumpets, sprang a battery of scarlet flowers.

As I photographed them, I found myself considering the cactus' role in the desert.

When the poet says

This is the dead land
This is cactus land

we feel his desolation. Yet for five hundred miles I had been walking past cacti and they had left no positive impression. They had not been a source of wonder like the flowers. They had not dragged at my feet like the sand or lifted my heart like the sunsets. Somehow they had hardly touched my life.

I had certainly noticed each new species. First there had been the striking saguaros, towering up twenty feet and more. Sometimes their fluted spires rose straight and simple, with little thumbs nubbing off. Sometimes they forked, and stood with arms raised in stiff and stylized supplication. Then, along the Colorado, there had been the untidy candelabra that looked as though a bunch of prickly green sausages had been stuck haphazardly by their ends onto an invisible core. In the Mojave I had found comic little brown porcupine-footballs that often sprouted puffs of white cotton. But as the novelty of each new species wore off they became an almost unnoticed item in the desert landscape.

There had been exceptions of course. Ever since Mexico I had been passing "beavertails." Their pimply green "paddles" made them the dullest cacti of all. Until they flowered. Then their cup-shaped blooms, porcelain-fine, blazed out in glorious splashes of vivid magenta. One radiant cluster, alone in deathliest Death Valley, had stopped me in my tracks. Then there had been the evening and morning at a Mojave night camp when the low sun, setting and rising, had turned the prickles of a mixed cactus grove into a galaxy of contorted halos. But, by and large, cacti had been something so inert that after five hundred miles they had left no impression positive enough to justify the poet's desolation. Until they flowered, they were there—and that was about all.

As I put my camera away after photographing the red trumpets in the rock gully, I felt vaguely uneasy. It seemed wrong—almost sinful—that such symbols of the desert had become something hardly more likely to catch my eye than the drainage gratings in a city gutter.

Sometimes the new faces that the desert showed me were variations on old themes.

It lay at the edge of the road, almost invisible in the fading light. I am still not sure what stopped me treading on it. Perhaps I saw a slight movement. Perhaps I heard the faint buzz. In any case, I pulled up short, a pace and a half from trouble.

The snake was barely a foot long and no thicker than my little finger. It lay in tensed curves, its fingernail of a rattle raised and vibrant. Even when I bent down I could hear only the same faint fly-buzz that had come from the pile of timber at Saratoga Spring. I peered closer, wondering if it really was a sidewinder. I had been hoping for a chance to see their distinctive, half-sideways movement.

And suddenly I realized that even in the first shock I had not been afraid. Only curious. I knew the bootlace at my feet was just as dangerous as the diabolical creature that two months earlier had straddled the Wetback Trail; but would I be feeling so calm if it had been as big? I wasn't sure. I could only hope it was familiarity and not mere diminutiveness that had removed the fear.

This was the third rattlesnake I had met since Death Valley. Twice in the Panamints I had almost trodden on small specimens. Each time I had experienced only a little fear. Each time I had allowed the snake to crawl away unharmed.

"Why kill them?" Matt Ryan had said at Emigrant Ranger Station when I told him about the four rattlers along the Colorado and the one at Saratoga Spring. "If you leave them alone they won't do you any harm. They were one of America's earliest national symbols, you know. Not attackers, but venomous in defense. They're gentlemen: they'll give you warning if you give them half a chance. And they have their part to play in the balance of nature. Kill them off, and you disturb all sorts of things. Our policy in the Monument is to let them be. Out in the blue, I mean. Around buildings it's different of course, or where there's kids. But the dangers are exaggerated, you know."

"Yes, I gather not too many people are actually killed by rattlers?" I asked.

"I'm not sure about the exact figure, but I think the total of recorded deaths in California history adds up to somewhere around five.* Even then, there's almost always been some contributory factor—extreme youth or age, heart trouble, or something. So we don't kill them. After all, we're trying to preserve a corner of America as the white man found it. The men at the top of the Park System always have that aim in mind. And the white man found rattlesnakes. People try to tell us it's not worth the risk. But hell, since the Monument was created in 1933 we haven't had a single case of snakebite. There've been close shaves of course, but nobody's been bitten, let alone died. And if we don't kill them inside the Monument, why outside? Away from people, I mean."

Matt's argument made sense. So I had allowed the next two rattlesnakes I met to escape. And I had felt good.

---

*Actually, Matt was underestimating slightly. Laurence Klauber, in his exhaustive two-volume *Rattlesnakes*, records that in California in the fourteen years 1931–1944, rattlers caused 19 human deaths. He estimates the average death rate at 2 or 3 per year, in a population of 13 million. The rate is so low that Matt Ryan's argument remains unaffected.

Now, as I stood looking down at the little bootlace with its vibrating rattle, I realized that early in The Walk rattlesnakes had worried me more than I had cared to admit. In the first month or so, rustling branches under my sleeping bag had given me several uneasy moments. But now I accepted rattlers as part of the desert. I would never collect them, as some people do, pushing ten or twenty into a sack and carrying the prize slung over one shoulder. But at least I could more or less live with them.

The snake still stood its ground. I flicked some sand and it began to retreat. Its body moved in wide, exaggerated curves that carried it forward with a peculiar semi-crabwise motion, as if an invisible force was diverting it at an angle from the path it wanted to travel. I watched it go, knowing that at last I had been lucky enough to see a sidewinder.

The snake disappeared into a bush and I walked on up the road, oddly pleased with myself. Stage by stage, as was its way, the desert had taught me something. When I killed those early rattlesnakes I could have justified myself with a score of reasons. But the "reasons" would have been excuses. I knew now that what drove me to kill was plain, ordinary, understandable fear.

Sometimes the desert's "new" faces were old features seen from a fresh angle.

As I ate lunch one day I glimpsed, close up, the heedless cruelty that lies hidden behind nature's "peacefulness." A leopard lizard emerged from a bush, chewing reflectively on a grasshopper. The grasshopper kicked and the lizard let go. The mangled insect jerked about on the sand. The lizard, taking its time, repossessed it. The performance was repeated once, twice, three times. Finally the grasshopper summoned dying reserves and with its one remaining leg leaped into a bush. The lizard moved forward five or six inches, closed its eyes—and fell asleep.

Another day, I sat beside the road, a little muddleheaded from the sun. Around me the desert stretched flat and empty.

And then, as I rested, I became conscious that it was not empty at all: it teemed with grasshoppers. They were small creatures, so small that they escaped the casual naked eye. I focused my binoculars on the stony road, as close up as I could. And like Alice stepping through the looking glass, I found myself in a different world.

It was a torrid, glaring, shadowless world. Across its "boulder-strewn" landscape a steady pilgrimage moved uphill, upwind, and into the sun. No terrible urgency drove the pilgrims forward. There was just a general I'll-move-on-when-I-want-to, this-sun-is-so-hot, we'll-get-there-sometime sort of attitude. They came in an irregular but continuous stream, rarely jumping, just crawling and resting, crawling and resting. At rest, they lapsed into torpor, all facing the same way, like ships anchored in a tideway.

They came in a hundred shapes and sizes and colors and conformations. Some were small and some were very small. Some had obvious wings and some did not. Some were tapered aft and some were blunt. But they all had stupid grasshopper heads, as stupid in their compressed way as a giraffe's.

There were undistinguished gray ones with pale blue movie-actress eyes. There were battleship-gray ones with tropical dazzle-paint finish. There were brown ones, bravely mottled with yellow and red and blue. And some were hot cinnamon all over.

Once, a blue-eye cut, woman-like, across the bows of a resting battleship-gray, brushing his foreleg as she passed. The battleship-gray dreamily raised the leg. He held it high for ten seconds, then lowered it partway. Twenty seconds later he lowered it almost to the ground. After a full minute, still with the detachment of a drug addict, he put it down.

I was wondering whether the afternoon sun accounted for his muzziness when I became conscious of its heat on my exposed neck. I tilted back my hat and lowered the binoculars.

Around me, the desert once more stretched flat and empty.

But the desert did not always give even a superficial appearance of emptiness.

I was walking northward along the dirt road. All around stretched sand and stones and creosote bushes. Apart from the road, there had been no sign of man for several hours. And then I came to a clearly distinguishable object. It stood alone and aloof, a dozen feet off the road. It was pitless and therefore useless. Its door stood open, revealing all. It was, exactly as large as life, an ordinary old-fashioned wooden privy.

Sometimes the desert's new faces were new in every way, though I could not always say what it was that created the newness.

The last morning I would be following the road, I woke at sunrise to find the air cool, almost cold. I had camped at dusk on a high plateau. Now, in the first sunlight, I saw snow-filled gullies less than a mile away. It was the closest I had been to snow since Mexico, closer even than above Death Valley. And again the snow kindled that odd excitement.

I got up and shook my sleeping bag. And there on the road, six feet from my bed, so freshly imprinted in thick dust that I half expected to find the cause still strolling down the road, I saw a perfect set of bobcat tracks. The low sun floodlit their indentations in sharp relief. As in a coarse-grained photograph, each speck of dust had value. I could almost hear the animal padding past while I slept.

After breakfast I walked on northward along the road. The bobcat tracks preceded me. The plateau that the road cut across was not a particularly beautiful place: just a rolling tableland with dark, buttony junipers dotting the pale green sagebrush. But some special quality in the light gave it a quickening vividness.

I turned a corner. A pair of junipers, one on each side of the road, framed a perfect picture. There was nothing very special about it, I suppose. Nothing that will quite go into words. There was no bobcat, no glorious splash of color, no sweeping panorama. Just the dark needles of the tree standing out in silhouette against the pale dust of the road. And a narrow view beyond. The view had a subtle, indefinite balance that was intensified by the vivid light. And away to the left, closer than ever, hung the snow-filled gullies. That was all.

I was standing still, devouring every detail of the scene, when for some reason I remembered that it was Monday. Back in San Francisco another weekend was over. All around the world people were pouring back into their squirrel cages.

And all at once I understood how lucky I was. For the first time I saw quite clearly that what mattered in The Walk were the simple things—snow and vivid light and sharp-grained bobcat tracks. My exhilaration swelled up and overflowed. And when at last I walked on past the two juniper trees toward the far side of the plateau I found I was feeling sorry for any man who was not free to abandon whatever futility detained him and to walk away into the desert morning with a pack on his back.

In the final hundred miles of desert I found only one permanently occupied habitation.

Marble Canyon was a stark place. Even in bright sunlight, an air of forlorn disuse hung over the cluster of pit hoists and wooden shacks that were strung out along the dirt road. But beside one shack stood a van; and, on the edge of a circle of whitewashed stones, a pair of neatly painted signs:

GREER and BEALS
STOP and PAN GOLD

Beneath them, a rectangle of unpainted plywood added, in rough script:

LEARN TO PAN GOLD. YOU GET FROM 2 TO 6 NUGGETS IN EACH PAN. $1.00 IN GOLD FOR EACH $1.00 YOU SPEND.

The door of the shack stood ajar. I knocked.

A long, weather-beaten face with a five-inch goatee appeared in the doorway. "Afternoon, friend," said a cheerful southern voice. Pale blue eyes smiled at me. Flowing gray hair hung down over thin shoulders.

"I wonder if you could tell me what the country's like down toward Eureka Valley?" I asked.

"Not sure I can be too much help about that," said the man. "But come right in, come right in. Coffee? Rather have tea? Sure, sure. Always keep plenty o' tea in the place. My name's Greer, Walter Greer."

We shook hands. Greer had long, sensitive fingers. His hands were not gnarled and calloused like a miner's, and he wore a thin, fine-check shirt with button-down collar. It had been carefully ironed.

The three-room shack was brightly furnished and very clean. "Couldn't live in one of those filthy bachelor cabins," said Greer as he put water on the stove. "Nossir, wash my dishes up right after every meal."

Over tea and cookies I asked again about the country ahead. For the first time since Mexico I had no large-scale map, and the inadequate one covering Eureka Valley left me vaguely uneasy.

"No, 'fraid I can't tell you much about that country. It's hell's own dry down in Eureka, that's for sure. But I can't walk far these days so I don't know the country worth a damn."

"Oh, how long have you been here then?"

"Only three years. I'm more of a fisherman than a miner. Fished with rod and line all over these United States, I have. Even made money out of it sometimes. Before that I drove a bus for twenty-seven years. St. Louis–Chicago run. Three million miles without an accident. No, when it comes right down to it, I guess you could say I'm not much of a miner."

He took a long draft of tea. "Done plenty of other things though. Born and raised in Arkansas, I was. Ma died, and Pa married again when I was eleven. Three weeks with my new Ma and I quit. Moved about a whiles, then joined the Merchant Navy. Sailed 'round the world twice, saw a hundred and sixty-three countries. Five years I stayed in the Navy, including the First World War. Afterwards I came back and settled down. Married, two kids, and drove a bus, like I said. But in 1944 I had to quit 'cause of arthritis. Crippled, I was. Hands all doubled up, and I had to move my legs with my arms. Look, I'll show you."

He went over to a drawer, rummaged, and brought out a snapshot. It was only just possible to recognize him. His body was emaciated and bent almost double, his face drawn and shrunken.

"Doctor sent me down to Arizona, and the desert soon fixed me. Yessir, the desert soon fixed me up. I drew a pension—enough to live on. Things went fine for a whiles, then I ran into more trouble. Six major operations in six months. Took out most of my guts, they did. Half my colon's gone, and I don't have any stomach muscles left, just skin. They said I couldn't live through it. But when the crisis came and I felt myself beginning to slip away I said to myself, 'Greer, don't be a damned fool! You've got twenty more years of good fishing to come yet.' And I pulled through. There's a lot to this willpower business, you know. If a man wants something badly enough he can usually get it.

"I fished all over afterwards. Mexico, Florida, New England, Canada, Alaska, everywhere. Bought that 1949 Ford cabover you saw outside. Designed for parcels' service, it was, but I had had it specially fitted out. The wife came along at first, but after a while she said she was fed up with that kind o' living. Wanted cities and parties and all that damn nonsense. So I sent her home. Saw her again after a year and a half. Next time it was two and a half years. I walked in and told her, 'Either you come with me in the cabover or you give me a divorce. You've got an hour to make up your mind.' So she came. For three months. Then she said, 'Get yourself a woman if you must, but take me back home.' 'Take you home?' I said, 'What's the matter with a bus?' 'But what about my clothes?' 'I'll mail 'em on,' I said. So I put her on the bus and she's still at home and looks after the house and the restaurant and mails on my pension checks. She's all right really, I know I can trust her . . . Mind you, I'd had the cabover fitted out real nice. Drink up that last cup o' tea and I'll show you."

The inside of the cabover looked like a fishing tackle store. Reels and tackle stood on ledges. Wobblers hung festooned like Christmas decorations. A thicket of rods flourished under the roof and sprouted in corners. Above the driver's seat was pinned a snapshot gallery: Walter Greer with fish beside the ocean, Walter Greer with fish beside mountain creeks, Walter Greer with fish beside desert lakes.

"I'm only sixty-four," said Greer as he demonstrated the two let-down bunks. "And there's still plenty of fishing left in me. A heap of places I want to go yet. Mind you, I've been in every state in the union already. Look . . ." He waved a hand. Every window was garnished with state stickers. They seemed to include about sixty-two out of the fifty.

"It's three years now since I bought a partnership in this mine. Thought I'd like the change. Had quite a time with rattlers at the start. This canyon's full of 'em. Killed forty-seven the first year. I can't work too hard on the mine 'cause of my operations; not supposed to lift more than ten pounds, but I do of course. And I pick up the odd dollar now and then by going to old-timer meetings and panning gold. Death Valley Forty-Niner meetings and the like. They go for this long-hair business, you know. Keeps the tourists happy. And once in a while a car comes through here. That's why I put those signs up." We had climbed down from the cabover and were standing out in the sunshine.

"I wonder if you'd mind if I took some photographs of you panning gold?" I asked.

"Sure, sure. Just wait while I get my miner's helment and fix the carbide lamp on it."

I took a few shots of him sitting under the signs, swirling nuggets around a prospecting pan. He had a row of cans set up for customers, each with its supply of sand and a fragment of gold. It was very bogus and rather pathetic, quite unlike the man as he really was.

A black-and-white cat kept getting into the act, rubbing affectionately against Greer's leg. "She gets thin like this eating lizards," he said, fondling her under the chin. "But she can move fast enough. You should see her catching bats on the roof of the cabover."

"What do you do about water?" I asked as we walked back to the shack.

"Haul my own drinking water in. Just pick some up every time I drive into town. And I save every drop of rainwater from the roof. Collect it in an underground tank. I've never run short, all the time

I've been here. Mind you, I'm careful not to waste any."

We went back indoors. "Yeah, three years I've been up here now. Longest I've stayed in one place since I left St. Louis. It's been OK, but I've been trying to sell for quite a while now. I'd like to be out this summer and back at my fishing. Mind you, I don't figure to quit the desert. Nossir. But there's a whole stack of lakes, and the Colorado too. It doesn't look like this place'll be easy to sell though. One bunch of guys said they were interested and brought along seven thousand silver dollars in sacks. They wouldn't take the dough into the bank with me though. Wanted the deal signed and sealed first. Said the bank might ask questions. 'So might I,' I said. 'Where d'you get the stuff, anyways?' 'Got it in a deal, as protection against inflation,' said one of them. 'Course I knew it wasn't no protection. Only gold's protection. And what chance would I have stood of getting the money to a bank? They all had thirty-eights strapped to their belts. So I turned it down."

"After that I tried to run an ad in the *Wall Street Journal*. They wouldn't take it at first. Wanted banker's references and all that guff. Even when I sent the references they still said no. So I wrote saying I wasn't a phony promoter, just a worn-out old miner who had to sell. And I got the nicest letter back from them. Yessir, good paper that *Wall Street Journal*, mighty good paper. Had a whole wad of replies to the ad and any number of people came out to look the place over. Several of 'em seemed real interested, but I've never quite managed to clinch a deal. Guess I must have talked too much."

Walter Greer looked up quickly. The skin around his blue eyes wrinkled, and his goatee bounced forward. "Yeah, guess I always talk too much . . ."

As its final surprise, the desert at last produced the wilderness of convention. For twenty miles it focused with pitiless clarity into the image we most of us conjure up at the word "desert," into the desert I had expected when I walked out beyond Imperial Dam nearly three months earlier: hostile and inhuman wasteland, a barren monotony of sand and heat—and thirst.

On the drive south to Mexico I had discovered, too late to do anything about it, that there was no water on the last leg at all, through Eureka Valley. But a burly Fish and Game Department Ranger named Mark Halderman had promised to put out a cache for me at some old cabins.

"You can't miss them," he had said. "There's a road runs across the north end of Eureka Valley and you'll find these cabins, two or three of them close together, up against the west side of the valley about two miles before you hit the road. Maybe three miles. I'm not sure. Anyway, there's a little side road runs out to them. You can't miss it."

"How far would you say the cabins were, the way I'll be going, from the last water in Marble Canyon?"

"Gee, I'm not too sure. I've never been around that way myself. Let's see, the last water'll be at old man Greer's place in Marble Canyon. Oh, at a guess I'd say fifteen miles. Can't be more than twenty. Anyway, I'll have water in one of those cabins by the first week in May at the latest, don't you worry about that."

But I did worry. Mark Halderman had impressed me as an experienced and thoroughly reliable man. But I would have worried if an archangel had put out the cache. The cabins were not marked on my small-scale map, and they might not be easy to find. There were always people too, like the rock hound at Saratoga Spring who had boasted of having taken a full bottle from a Death Valley cache. One way and another, I found it hard not to worry.

Soon after I left Walter Greer's cabin and headed down Marble Canyon, away from the road, my vague disquiet began to harden into something stronger.

It began when I lost my map. When my hand found emptiness in the shirt pocket, I stopped dead. All day I had been uneasy because the map was inadequate. But now I felt like a miner without his lamp.

I slipped off my pack and headed back the way I had come. I knew I was probably wasting my time. Gusts of wind were funneling down the canyon. The map, cut down to postcard size to save weight, would hardly stay where it had fallen. But I kept on going, backtracking my footprints and realizing for the first time just how much I had grown to rely on maps.

In twenty minutes I reached the place I had last checked the route. The wind was stronger now, and there was no sign of the little scrap of paper. I hurried back down the canyon. With each step my disquiet hardened.

Beyond the loss of the map, nothing had actually happened. At least, nothing that amounted to much. An hour earlier a thin snake had raced past, almost between my legs. The moment I had time to think, I knew it was harmless. But, in spite of my new attitude to rattlesnakes, the speed and suddenness had momentarily scared me. And ripples of fear take time to subside. I suppose there were other things as well, mere nothings in themselves: gaunt canyon walls, fading light, doubts about Mark Halderman's water cache, Walter Greer's snake stories, even gusts of wind that blew cold on my back where the pack usually pressed. As I hurried back down the canyon I thought, "If I *did* get bitten by a rattler now, the pack would seem one hell of a long way off." The snake kit never left my shorts' pocket; but I would need water and a sleeping bag to tide me over. All the way down the canyon I felt naked and unprotected. When I saw the pack again, leaning against a boulder, it was like coming home on a winter's evening and finding a log fire burning in the hearth.

The map search had wasted forty minutes. When darkness fell I was only just in sight of the canyon mouth. Beyond it stretched a blank. A gray-black nothingness.

As I cooked dinner I tried to forget that first impression of Eureka Valley. I kept telling myself that I had memorized the contours of the map so thoroughly that its loss meant nothing. But when I slid into my sleeping bag and went through the nightly routine of putting my "office" (spectacles, pen, and notebook) into the bedside boots, I felt acutely aware that a map was missing from the files.

When I woke next morning the disquiet had more or less gone.

Then, an hour after breakfast, I walked clear of

the last buttresses of Marble Canyon, and the full expanse of Eureka Valley opened out before me. Boulders lay half buried in the sand, like gravestones of a dead civilization. Wraith-like smoke bushes barely altered the gray light of a lowering sky. And a pall seemed to lie over everything, as if the dust of ages had settled on the bottom of a huge, ancient coffin.

But what struck me most was sheer size.

As I stood at the mouth of Marble Canyon and looked out over the gray waste I had to cross, I felt an even greater sense of brooding immensity than I had done at the entrance to Death Valley. Yet, compared with Death Valley, Eureka is a pudding basin. Perhaps it was just that the loss of the map had left me unprepared; or perhaps I was overconscious that in that bone-dry sink I was depending on water cached at an ill-defined point, unmarked on any map, by someone I hardly knew. But whatever the causes, the fact remains that as I walked out into the pallid gray dust bowl and began to crunch across the rubble and stones that fanned out from the mouth of Marble Canyon, I felt very small, very fragile, and very unprotected.

Almost at once I began to peer ahead for the cabins. The evening before, I had come perhaps ten miles from Walter Greer's place; and Mark Halderman had said it could hardly be more than twenty from there to the cabins. So with luck they would soon appear.

I had walked barely a mile when I saw, far ahead, two black dots that might have been roofs. Half an hour later I knew they were not.

At first the walking was fairly easy, along a gentle stony slope. Then the washes began: deep-cut ravines with steep, crumbling sides. I bucked them like a coastal freighter in mid-Atlantic. Sweat trickled down my back. At the first halt I restricted myself to a single sip of water.

About 8:30 a second pair of dark blobs, still far ahead, raised my hopes again. Another half hour, and they too had become something still indefinite but definitely not cabins.

The washes deepened. I cut down the slope, away from the western hills. The valley floor, level and inviting from a distance, turned out to be soft and yielding sand. I plowed along like a prisoner dragging chains. The dusty desert closed about me. I began to wish I had been more sparing with the gallon of water I had carried away from Walter Greer's shack; that morning, by the time I left the mouth of Marble Canyon, I had used more than half of it.

To most people, thirst is as much a part of the desert as sand and cacti. Gaunt movie heroes, open-mouthed and sweat-lathered, stagger across endless sand dunes toward inevitable last-minute oases. I had taken care to avoid such dramatics. Since switching from Spartan water rationing to a drink-a-little-when-you-want-it economy I had only once been at all thirsty; and that had been through carelessness. One morning in the Panamint Mountains, banking on water at at least one of three marked springs, I had started the day with only a pint in my canteens. Eight hours later, high on the mountain, I had run the last few yards to an old cattle trough and the wonderful cool greenness it held. And that day had by desert standards been cool and pleasant.

Now, as I struggled northward along the floor of Eureka Valley, the weather was neither cool nor pleasant. Gray clouds pressed heavily down. The air felt hot and sticky. As I walked, I made rough calculations. My bare half gallon of water would take me to the cabins in comfort; but if I missed them or found no water there, I faced at least another twenty bone-dry miles. I had known that when I started of course. But then success had seemed certain. Now, dragging my feet through the soft sand, I was not so sure.

I trudged on. Without warning, I walked onto a stretch of hard, flood-scoured mud. The relief was the same as you get from driving onto a freeway after hours of potholed corduroy. Half a mile, and the soft sand was back, sucking at my feet. I allowed myself another sip of water before struggling on. The gray clouds thinned and the sun broke through. The heat sharpened; but the dust still lay over everything like a gray blanket.

Half an hour later I hit a new stretch of mud-baked freeway. And almost immediately I saw, far ahead, a road winding along under the western hills. Even through binoculars I could see no cabins. But there was no doubt about the road. My watch said 10:30. I found it hard to believe that only four and a half hours had passed since I struck camp.

One narrow road, of course, gave no guarantee of water. But it was enough to dispel my doubts. I halted. To save water, just in case, I lunched on two eggs that Walter Greer had given me. Then I slept briefly under a bush. At eleven o'clock I started walking again.

Ten minutes later I saw the two cabins.

It was exactly noon when I reached them. They huddled close together. They were squat and ugly. They looked like the portals of Heaven.

Beside the second one stood an old silver trailer, and on its door fluttered a sheet of paper:

> Colin: Your water bottles are inside.
> Mark.

I opened the door. Heat beat out at me like the blast of a flamethrower. I stepped inside. Old magazines littered everything—floor, bench, bunk, windowsill, table. But on the edge of the table stood two gallon-size wine bottles. A note guarded them:

> Please leave these water bottles as they are. This is a scheduled stop for a gentleman traveling afoot—he is depending on the water being here.
> Thanks.
> Mark Halderman.
> Big Pine.

Both bottles were full.

Half an hour later, quenched, I lay on the bunk, reading.

Among the litter of magazines I had come across a tattered *Saturday Evening Post* dated August 13, 1955. A "box" on the cover had caught my eye.

Tales of the Death Valley Rangers:
FOOLHARDY TOURISTS
vs. THE DESERT

The title of the lead article read:

DEATH LURKS IN THE DESERT

In the photograph above it, Matt Ryan was shepherding tourists along a paved road in Death Valley. The article was full of stories about travelers who had died hideous deaths from heatstroke and thirst.

It made interesting reading.

Next afternoon I climbed at last to the head of a narrow pass. It was the end of the desert. Beyond, the mountains began.

I rested on a granite slab and looked back across Eureka Valley. It was still flat, immense, and deathly gray. But far beyond it I could make out the blue peaks of the Panamints. It seemed a more fitting memory to carry away.

Three months earlier I had approached the desert grimly, accepting the conventional image of sand and cacti, thirst and monotony. I was carrying away a glorious *pasticcio* of memories.

The sand and the cacti were there of course. Even the thirst. But they were swamped by the hummingbirds and dragonflies and coyote yowls, by tamarisk trees and warm granite slabs, by mountains and canyons and broad washes, by heat and morning freshness, by glare and evening softness.

I remembered waking beside the Colorado to see the sky filled with those soaring white birds. I remembered standing above the Devil's Elbow while the blue river swirled past a thousand feet below. I remembered watching a grasshopper beside my campfire and seeing it jump without warning clear through the flames and land, apparently unsinged, on the far side. I remembered picking up the body of a lizard from between two hinged pieces of metal and turning the corpse this way and that to catch the light and thinking that the markings looked as brilliant and the body as plump and solid as if the poor little thing had still been alive; and I remembered how the corpse had opened one eye and looked straight into mine and how, the moment the first glazed stupidity of waking had passed, the wriggling body had twisted free and scuttled off like a lizard out of hell.

I remembered echoes of distant places. Back near the Mexican border I had walked one hot afternoon through an Indian reservation. There was an open space, a meeting place of some kind, where the bare red soil had been worn hard and smooth. Along one side, a low building with a deep veranda stood gaunt and unpainted. The place slumbered, grateful for the kindness of the sun. But the sun had sucked away the land's vitality. I might have been back in Kenya. I should hardly have been surprised if a Kipsigis herdsman had stepped out from the shadow of the veranda, stretched, then stopped to stare at me, standing on one shiny black leg and holding his blanket tightly about him. Then there had been Ira's Hereford cattle that somehow subsisted beside the Colorado. The moment they saw me they had streaked away with tails held rigid and horizontal, like fronds of petrified seaweed. I wondered how one of the slow, conservative farmers of Hereford, on the English-Welsh border, would have reacted to the sight. The contrast between the ridges and washes of the Colorado and the lush pastureland of his own Wye Valley would amaze him; but no more than would the gulf between these frantic steeplechasers and his own slow, conservative stock from which they were descended. Back in the sanctuary of his village pub he would punctuate the calls of "Time, gentlemen, please!" with the triumphant, singsong finale to his story: ". . . but they all had white faces, I tell you—they all had white faces."

But most of all I remembered the flowers. I remembered the two ethereal orbs floating above the sand beside my Mojave water cache. I remembered the translucent mauve brandy glass that had shocked and delighted me with its five scarlet-feather inlays. And out in the dusty desolation of Eureka Valley I had that very morning seen a lone "buttercup" that merited a citation for courage. But it was not the individual flowers that really mattered, or even the way they thronged a slope, thick and varied as a baseball crowd. What I should never forget was the staggering aggregate, the incessant repetition, the endlessness. At Imperial Dam I had wondered how far back the flowers could stretch. Now, after six hundred miles, I knew.*

It seemed right that the flowers had merged into a single, all-embracing idea. For the essence of my memories lay in something beyond physical detail. Back in San Francisco I had often been puzzled by

---

*I had recognized all along that I was lucky to have chosen a wet year. But I did not understand quite *how* lucky.

"Most years," a geographer friend told me later, "those foothills of the Panamints that you saw 'covered with a soft green nap' would have been ungodly brown. And you might have walked all day down that Mojave Wash and seen perhaps a dozen flowers. Frankly, the odds are pretty long against coming away from the desert with the memory of a continuous flower garden."

desert talk, by some spell the desert seemed to exert over people. I had wondered why they rushed down for vacations, kept going back again and again, and in the end sometimes moved there to live. Now I understood. But I found it hard to explain how—or even what—I understood. It had something to do with the fragrance of wild lavender crushed beneath my sleeping bag, with the vigor of a dusty mesa after rain. It had something to do with openness, mile after mile, day after day. Mornings came into it too, with gray hillsides touched into red life by the rising sun. Then there were the evenings: the burned rim of a western sky at sunset; hills deepening to blue-black at twilight. Perhaps the evenings most of all. God is light, we are told, and hell is outer darkness. But look at a desert mountain stripped bare by the sun, and you learn only geography. Watch darkness claim it, and for a moment you may grasp why God had to create Satan—or man to create both.

It is with such moments of insight that the desert imprisons people.

Walter Greer was not the only one. Matt Ryan and his wife, Rosemary, had found at Emigrant Ranger Station a peace that left them calm and almost skeptical about nuclear explosions over the way at Frenchman's Flat. I had met others too. A tall young man who found the canyons of Death Valley at once a challenge and a place to forget his broken marriage. A retired mailman, a philosopher, whose trailer-and-fishing life beside the Colorado had rescued him from the rat race that caused his heart attack. ("Two years ago I couldn't walk two blocks. Now I can pack a one-hundred-pound sack of spuds.") These people had all found what they wanted in the desert. I no longer remembered very clearly what Chickenhouse Smith looked like; but I knew more certainly than ever that he was a wise man. He might not know how to manipulate a mortgage; but with his "five or six homes like this, all across the desert" he did not need to know. And he had said, "Don't fight the desert. Just learn to get along with it." In their different ways, all these people had found what they wanted.

I had found what I wanted too. I am a slow understander, and I knew the deep effects would appear only in the perspective of time. But the surface detail looked good. My body had been refined by twenty pounds; it was all bone and whipcord. I had relearned such simple delights as being able, when I was hot and tired, to stand naked in the breeze. And there had been moments when the desert captured me utterly. I remembered a remote valley (wild burros won't drag the name from me) in which I had daydreamed about building a cabin, perhaps even a house. I had found a place with shade and water and a winding access road, even a ready-made airstrip. There were salt flats and black lava strips and encircling mountains with immense harmonic sweep. But best of all there was the evening race among the peaks. First, long fingers of shadow pulled a blue cover across the valley floor. Then, slowly, the shadow enveloped the mountains. One by one, it snuffed out the sunlit peaks. I had watched spellbound as a race developed for the honor of being the last pink pinnacle. After the race had been lost and won—won by an outsider lying far back to the north—I dreamed about sitting on the veranda of my cabin (or would it be a real house?) and watching this spectacle every evening.

Now, resting in the pass above Eureka Valley, I knew my cabin was a castle in Spain. But I also knew that I would never again wonder at the way people fall so often and so utterly under the desert's insidious and altogether delightful spell.

I turned at last and looked westward through the pass toward the mountains.

A week earlier, near the crest of the Panamints, I had glimpsed the Sierra Nevada. Peak after snow-capped peak they had receded, a remote white world of their own. Now, the nearest peaks stood close and immediate. But the tapering line to the north was blocked by the huge bulk of White Mountain. It looked immense and forbidding. Much more forbidding than the packed contours had foretold when I planned which way to climb it, back in my apartment in San Francisco. And much more enticing too.

I looked back once more at the desert. Then I walked westward down the pass toward my first big American mountain.

CHAPTER

6

OVER WHITE MOUNTAIN

One of the deeply satisfying things about a mountain—almost any mountain—is the way it can at the same time belong exclusively to so many people.

During the second half of June, White Mountain belonged to me. I knew that it also belonged to at least two other men, but that made no difference.

Even before I climbed up out of the desert I knew that the mountain belonged to Doug Powell. I had run into Doug back in San Francisco during the hectic month of planning. Our chance meeting turned out to be a cornucopic stroke of luck. Doug was a highly practical geographer, and once he had overcome a natural distrust of The Walk he poured out information like a computer. He reeled off temperatures, humidity, and rainfall for localities most Californians have never heard of. He gave me first-hand reports on desert springs and remote mountain passes. And before long I discovered that he was one of those rare and invaluable experts who always admits when he's not sure of his facts.

I suppose I should have recognized back in San

Francisco how Doug felt about White Mountain—by what he withheld rather than what he stated (though his mastery of understatement almost qualifies him for British citizenship). I should have caught the significance of his "Oh yes, there's a considerable view from the peak." But I was too busy burrowing for facts to appreciate overtones. I detected them only when I met Doug again during a three-week rest period I spent at the foot of the mountain, waiting for the heaviest snow to melt.

All through those three weeks, Doug kept turning up at odd times and places. I began to understand why a good friend of his had told me: "Doug Powell's the sort of man you find yourself expecting to meet unexpectedly halfway up a remote mountain. He'll greet you most amiably, just as if you'd bumped into each other on Main Street. After a pleasant five-minute chat he's liable to wander off with a casual 'Well, see you later maybe.' But the thing about Doug is that he very likely *will* see you later."

Doug, of course, would recoil from any suggestion that he "owned" White Mountain, even in part. But that does not alter the true situation: his unstaked claim rests on a solid foundation. No man alive knows more than he does about that untamed flake of the earth's crust.

Doug first saw the mountain when he was sixteen. That July, he had camped with a party of other boys high on the western slopes of the Sierra Nevada. One day they made the long climb to a fourteen-thousand-foot peak. At last Doug scrambled onto the summit. Far below him spread the vast brown desert he had expected. But fifty miles away, blocking his eastern view, there reared up out of the desert a massive and utterly unexpected mountain range. Its crest rose as high as the peak on which he stood, and its entire length was capped with snow. Doug moved a little apart from the other boys and sat down on a rock. For a long time he gazed in silence at the huge bulk of the range, at its glistening snowcap and dark plunging slopes. Then he stood up and walked over to the party's leader. "They're called the White Mountains," said the man. "But nobody seems to know much about them." And in that moment a geographer was born.

Twenty-odd years have passed. They have produced a master's thesis on White Mountain and much more besides. Summer and winter, whenever he could, Doug has tramped over White Mountain's snowfields and rock slopes, up and down its ridges and steep valleys. His knowledge is all-embracing. There are moments when I feel he knows every time somebody kicks a stone out of place. Recently, a year after I had left the mountain, I showed him a night photograph of a campfire I had built at ten thousand feet. "Ah yes," said Doug. "Just beside the felled bristlecone pine at Eva Belle. That forked stick you used for cooking—the left one—was still standing when I passed by a couple of months back."

In exchange, the mountain has given Doug far more than an accumulation of facts, has taught him far more than geography. It has given him a deep comprehension of our world. It has helped him to understand not merely rocks and rivers, not merely birds and beasts, not merely people and their pursuits, but the subtle relationships, constantly changing, that bind them all together.

I knew I could not expect to meet Doug unexpectedly halfway up White Mountain. The day I started, he left on a trip to the Peruvian Andes. But I knew I should not often forget his co-ownership.

It was Doug himself who told me about the other "owner."

Along the narrow summit plateau of the mountain, the University of California operates three high-altitude research stations. One is at 10,000 feet, one at about 12,500, and one—rarely open—on the summit. At Number Two Station, alone all year except for an assistant in late summer, lives Bill Roche. Cut off from the world, battling all winter against hurricane winds and arctic temperatures, he tends a sizable menagerie of experimental animals and moves about the barren plateau on foot or in tracked snow vehicles. In five years he has been off the mountain for only two or three brief vacations.

"If Bill Roche decides to do anything to help you," said Doug Powell, "he'll go all the way. But quite a few strangers wander up in summer, and he naturally gets a bit fed up with interruptions. If you like"—and I recognized the suggestion as an honor—"if you like you can mention my name, though I'm not sure it'll do any good."

Mountains that are big enough and strong enough do not generate jealousy. I have never seen Doug Powell and Bill Roche together; but I am fairly sure they not only tolerate each other—they hold each other in considerable if reluctant respect.

I knew most of these things when I began to climb up out of the desert. And I acknowledged that these two men held prior claims to White Mountain. But for two weeks it was still "my" mountain.

White Mountain Peak is the culminating point of a long narrow range that thrusts up—aloof and improbable, like a reef from open sea—between the snowcapped Sierra massif and the rolling Lahontan desert. The western wall of the ridge sweeps up without check for ten thousand feet in a line of forbidding buttresses. On the east the slope is easier. As you stand in the desert, the huge bulk looms above in mysterious humps and bulges. Infant creeks twist and tumble from hidden valleys. As all good mountainsides should, it beckons and at the same time fills with awe.

It was up and along this slope that I climbed toward White Mountain Peak.

I suppose we all of us retain a reluctance to venture out beyond the safety of what we know. At the end of my three-week rest I discovered that part of me hesitated to wrench itself away from the familiar desert—the desert that four months earlier had been a stranger. But as soon as I began to climb up among the humps and bulges, my reluctance lost its edge.

I climbed slowly, stopping whenever I wanted to. Some days I walked for only two or three hours. Occasionally I followed faint trails that kept tapering away and leaving me to try and pick them up again by the feel of the gradient. More often I followed the map and my own inclinations. And as I climbed, the spell of the desert faded.

The first night, I camped in a desert canyon that echoed to the chatter of a mountain stream.

The second night, I slept in a little round frying pan of a sagebrush meadow. Junipers dotted the surrounding hills, like green-headed pins in a circle of pincushions. But in spite of the sage and junipers, it was not desert country. Next day, as I climbed among towering granite bluffs, I caught my first glimpse of the peak. Gray clouds swirled about a distant, snow-covered pyramid. It was remote, forbidding, intriguing.

The third night, I rolled out my sleeping bag among rocks and bushes. A marmot—fat and furry, like a child's teddy bear—perched on top of a boulder and chirped at me with incongruous bird song. Six hundred feet above, a snowbank clung to the crest of a ridge.

The fourth night, I knew I had finally left the desert behind.

The mystery of the desert is the mystery of distance. The sun strips everything to naked bone; only in distance is there haze and doubt. Beyond your flickering campfire stretches infinite blackness. Moonlight reveals immense, echoing vistas.

But the mystery of the forest is the mystery of suggestion. It fills you with the deepest kind of satisfaction—the kind that always leaves part of you unsatisfied. Even broad daylight never dispels all doubt. A stone rolls down a steep slope and you can only guess what set it in motion. A squirrel? A deer? A bear? Or nothing? Peering through the trees, you glimpse movement that is not a squirrel, might be a deer, might even be a bear—but for a moment was unquestionably something. At night, around your campfire, figures dance on tree trunks in obscure and tantalizing rhythms. Afterwards, moonlight cuts down through the trees and creates green, mysterious arenas. A memory stirs. You see again the backdrop that fascinated you, many years ago, in *Peter Pan* or *Babes in the Wood*. At the beginning of the scene, with lights so low that the unimportant figures on stage were mere shadows, the backdrop was magical. It promised tremendous trees or cavernous caves or enchanted fairy rings or all three at once or perhaps something quite different. In the play, they always spoiled it by bringing the lights slowly up until you could see that the shadowy shape was after all only a big tree or a large cave or an ordinary fairy ring; after that it could never be all three at once or something excitingly unexpected. But in a forest the lights are never brought up. Not until morning—and that is a different world.

I have written: "the mystery of the forest." I am not sure White Mountain supports anything that should be thought of as "forest." It is really, I suppose, a desert mountain. But it has moments that border on richness, and after the miles and months of true desert I reveled in its sparsely timbered slopes and well-watered little valleys.

That fourth night, I camped beside an aspen grove. A creek ran at my bedside. On its grassy bank a cluster of purple shooting stars poised ready to plunge from delicate stalks. If I walked twenty feet to a certain mossy boulder, I could smell wild strawberries. After dark, my campfire shadows danced minuets and sambas on the slender aspens. And back among the trees, moonlight created a cavernous cave or a Druid's cromlech or both at once or perhaps something quite different.

And on the fifth night, in stark and stony country high above the last meadow, I camped among snowdrifts and the oldest living things on earth.

The bristlecone pines that grow high on the eastern slopes of White Mountain reach an age of 4,500 years. This surpasses by more than a thousand years the known world record previously held by another California tree, the giant Sierra sequoia or redwood.

Living bristlecone pines are not impressive. They have none of the majesty of redwoods. A few reach seventy-five feet in height; but they are straggly, amorphous affairs. The majority never grow higher than thirty feet. In a grove of redwoods, a living bristlecone pine would pass unnoticed.

But the nobility of the dead trees transcends mere size. Every skeleton is a monument to age. From a squat nucleus that is less a dead tree trunk than an immense fossilized muscle there taper toward the sky a hundred anguished arms, smooth and suppliant and surrealist. The mellow brown wood, virtually indestructible under local conditions, is cracked into lines and knotted into pregnant curves. The eloquent dead live on among the silent living.

Death comes slowly to a bristlecone pine. An apparently lifeless skeleton may still support, halfway up one tapering arm, a single living sprig. In failing evening light I stood silent and sober before one such colossal wreck. Somewhere in that twisted structure the sap still ran. Yet when Christ died this tree had already passed the halfway mark along its course of life.

It was among the bristlecone pines that I found the log cabin of the old Eva Belle mine.

In my meanderings up the eastern slope I came across only three cabins. All three reflected the transitoriness of man's works.

The first, at the end of a dirt road, hardly above the desert, was little more than a shelter. The second, an abandoned forestry station at 9,500 feet, was a more solid affair; but already it belonged to the past. Doug Powell had told me that the place was still used for a month or two each summer by cattlemen who brought their herds up from the dry eastern valleys; but the buildings, though well constructed and in good repair, gave the impression of flotsam left high and dry on the banks of time. And they were not true mountain cabins. Their flat plank walls and green composition roofs would have fitted without discord into Walter Greer's desert canyon.

But the cabin at Eva Belle was different.

Squat and defiant, it crouched among snowbanks that still lingered beneath the bristlecone pines. On three sides, bare stony slopes swept up for a thousand feet. Snow hung along them in precarious terraces. Even in warm sunlight it was easy to picture the place in winter—sterile, bitter, and menacing.

The cabin stood at bay against the elements. It seemed to cling to the sloping ground like a limpet. Massive untrimmed logs protruded for a foot at each corner, as if to ensure against even an earthquake. Stones held down the low-pitched log roof.

In spite of the sunshine, the cabin stood aloof, lonely. As I walked into its clearing, a few gray birds objected to the intrusion in tones halfway between those of a crow and a plaintive lamb. On a nail in the cabin wall hung a heavy rusted frying pan. Inside, light percolated through the roof. It showed a bed frame, rough-hewn tables and benches, and a small iron stove. A broom lay on the dirt floor and there was soap in a cracked dish. But everything was thickly coated with the dust of disuse. The cabin would be a welcome haven in a storm, but that was all.

I went fifty yards down the slope, set up camp, and for the first time since Mexico melted snow for water.

From camp, the cabin regained its stature. Like the forestry station, it belonged to the past; but there was something more enduring about it—something even more solid than its stout walls—that I could not quite define.

Some time after midnight I came awake and opened my eyes. Moonlight streamed down into the little clearing. Wind was tossing the treetops like a sea. I looked up toward the cabin. Its low outline stood foursquare against dark trees and glistening snowbanks. High above, the skyline swept 'round in a cold, distant semi-circle.

An unexpected emotion stirred in me. England has no log-cabin tradition; it all happened too long ago. In the outposts of empire the cabin, in various forms, is still part of the crumbling present. But the log cabin is built into "grass roots" America. Every American child knows that Abe Lincoln was born and raised in a cabin like the Eva Belle. His background helped make him a great American symbol. Today, a presidential candidate might suppress Eva Belle origins, or transfer them to an underprivileged city block. But echoes of the tradition linger on. They even permeate creeping suburbia; the modern western supermarket likes to imply suggestions of rugged individualism by gluing mock Eva Belle logs along its low rancho walls.

I had for a long time recognized the role the log cabin played in carrying forward the American projection of Western culture. But it is one thing to recognize a symbol, quite another to feel it. And, without feeling, a symbol remains a husk. That night on White Mountain, with wind tossing the treetops and moonlight throwing deep shadows beneath the eaves of the Eva Belle, I understood for the first time something of the warmth and solidity the log cabin has contributed to the American heritage.

Cabins are not the only testimonial that White Mountain offers to the transitoriness of man's works.

America as a whole and California in particular are known as lands of boom and growth; but even California has its islands of bust and sag. Beside the Colorado, in the derelict ranches above Picacho, I had found an "island" that busted. White Mountain sagged—and is still sagging. Relics remain.

At the mouth of the canyon up which I started to climb the mountain, I found all that is left of White Mountain City—one small cairn-like smelter and the outlines of a few uncemented stone houses. At its zenith as a mining center, the population of the hamlet never exceeded a handful, and its main contribution to history is, oddly enough, political. Doug Powell told me the story. In the State senatorial election of 1861, White Mountain City precinct cast a total of 521 votes. These votes tipped the scales in a tight race between four leading contestants for two available seats. One disgruntled candidate, finding only a handful of miners living in the hamlet at the foot of White Mountain, checked the voting register. An investigation followed. One account of it reports: "A citizen who looked over the list was struck with the familiar appearance of some of the names, and finally ascertained that they had been copied from the passenger list of the steamer on which he had come from Panama to San Francisco." Justice prevailed. Two years after the election, the usurping senators were unseated.

After I had climbed above Eva Belle, I saw, away to the north, a small tilted tableland that I had already christened The Shepherds' Mecca. The tableland, at an elevation of more than twelve thousand feet, hangs precariously on the brink of a two-thousand-foot talus slope. In the 1890s, Doug Powell had told me, it formed the high point of a prodigious annual trek made by French sheepherders who had settled in the upper San Joaquin Valley. Every spring they drove their flocks eastward. By mid-summer they had moved into the High Sierra or the White Mountains. In August, as the climax of the pilgrimage, a few of them would drive their sheep up onto this apparently inaccessible tableland. By late October they were back in their San Joaquin homesteads, after a six-month trek of more than seven hundred miles. My White Mountain map, dated 1917, showed two foot trails angling up and across a precipitous talus slope near the main peak. "That's the way they brought their sheep down," Doug Powell had said. "How they did it is just about beyond me. There's almost no sign of the trails now, and it takes a man all his time to get across on his own."

A century has reduced White Mountain City to a few stones. After seventy years the French sheepherders' trails have almost vanished. And the process of sag goes on. It permeates the surrounding countryside. The northern end of White Mountain ridge penetrates across the boundary into Nevada. Now the laws of Nevada permit—often encourage—activities that are frowned upon in California and other states. Hence Reno and Las Vegas. But even the oldest of man's institutions has proved susceptible to White Mountain's brooding presence. A local paper recently reported the closure of an isolated establishment that had long been active just across the state line in the very shadow of the mountain. It quoted the outgoing owner as lamenting, not too surprisingly, "I guess it's just not a place for prostitution."

"Up on top," Doug Powell had warned, "it's never still."

And when I came up out of the last of the bristlecone pines onto the narrow summit plateau, I knew what he meant.

Down at Eva Belle, an hour earlier, it had been hot. The living trees stood as motionless as the dead. Snowbanks perspired in the sun.

Up on the plateau, it was as if a revolving stage had been turned. For minutes on end the wind might be no more than a brisk movement of cold air; then a disembodied iceberg would slap against my body, run through it, and pass on. Even on that barren waste—much more barren than most of the desert—I could hear the gusts coming. They rasped across the stones like a file.

At first my eye saw nothing but an expanse of brown stones undulating in curves so smooth that they might have been finished with sandpaper. But as I walked on I discovered little clumps of coarse grass. Here and there, a scrap of dwarf sage hugged the ground. Among the stones, so small that you had to bend down to see them, grew delicate little white and yellow and purple flowers. And over and between the flowers bustled a sparse but widespread population of beetles and spiders. The spiders in particular seemed to reflect the ceaseless struggle for existence. Faced by the looming, incomprehensible bulk of an Italian mountain boot, they did not scuttle for cover but stood at bay, pugnacious as a big league pitcher.*

I crossed half a mile of stony waste, climbed two snowdrifts, and turned north along a twisting jeep road.

When Doug told me that a road serviced the high-altitude research station, I was afraid its mere presence would destroy that compelling hostility you find in all high and treeless places. But perhaps hostility is too strong a word. Perhaps I mean superb arrogance, or merely the self-assurance of diamond beauty. The quality has something to do with bareness, something to do with cold, something to do with closeness to the sky and with immense distances, seen or unseen. Anyone who knows high places will recognize it.

That quality, whatever it is, swamped the tenuous fact of the jeep road. I felt myself responding to the plateau. The exhilaration of high places is as real—and as difficult to define—as their fascination. I suppose the one is the result of the other: but the chain of cause and effect is obscure. It is a biological fact that extreme altitude reduces the brain's efficiency: but it is a fact of experience that mountaintops exhilarate. Perhaps I am thinking only

---

*Later, when I told Doug Powell how the spiders had impressed me by their pugnacity, he murmured, "I think you may have been mistaken."

Translated, this meant, "Nonsense!"; but I still know how they looked to me.

of excitement, of the upsurge that follows achievement; for I have never stayed really high for more than a few days, and always there have been long intervals between visits. Perhaps the really experienced no longer feel exhilaration. On mountains, as in other fields, there are advantages to inexperience.

For two hours I walked north along the jeep road. The pyramid of the peak stood clear before me, six or seven miles away. It was no longer a remote and forbidding citadel, half obscured by swirling cloud. Outlined against blue sky, the rock glowed warm and brown. Snowfields sparkled. The pyramid was not merely approachable: it invited.

The road dipped. The peak sank from view. And at about six o'clock, in a shallow saucer that did little to shelter the cluster of buildings from the wind, I came to Number Two high-altitude research station.

I found Bill Roche in his kitchen. He was a spare, bespectacled man with a shock of anarchistic hair. There was about him nothing of the mountaineer, the hermit, or the oddball. Given a comb, he might have been the man who delivers your laundry.

"So you know Doug Powell, eh?" he said, unpacking some stores. "Did you stay at Number One Station last night?"

Number One Research Station—the lowest of the three—was ten miles back down the road at ten thousand feet. I explained that I had come up the eastern slope of the mountain and so avoided it.

"Oh, a *real* hiker?" said Bill Roche. He was silent for a moment. "Look, if you're going up to the peak you'd best use the summit station. But you can't make it tonight, you know. It's better than five miles from here, and quite a climb at the end. Why don't you stop over with us?"

"Well . . ."

"Sure you will. We can probably rustle up some food as good as anything you've got in your pack. A couple of visitors came up today and brought in these supplies. We're three for dinner as it is, so one more won't make any difference. Have a drink first, anyway. It's about time for one—and it'll help you make up your mind."

The visitors turned out to be two biochemists up to make animal experiments. The substitutes for my dehydrated potatoes and pemmican and melted snow turned out to be avocados and T-bone steaks and fresh raspberries and burgundy. After dinner we moved to the upper floor of the big Quonset hut. Outside its curved metal walls, the wind whistled faintly. Inside, our feet sank into thick carpet.

Bill Roche's friendly brown dog followed us upstairs. "Most intelligent animal I've ever known," said Bill. "She came up with a batch of other dogs for a series of experiments. Fifty injections. The others always snarled, but after the first few times Brownie just put her paw out and turned her head the other way. That was two years ago. She's been with me ever since."

"I guess you don't get too many people up here for company," I said.

"Well, sometimes I have an assistant. In summer, people often come up for experiments—and I get quite a few casual visitors. Some of them are pretty queer too. You know those granite outcrops that stick up all around here? Last year an electrical engineer from Los Angeles came up with his wife.

He stood and looked at the outcrops for a long time. 'Tell me,' he said at last. 'What did they put *those* there for?' "

I laughed. "But doesn't *any*body come up all winter?"

"Not often. The plateau is passable in a weasel—that's one of those light track vehicles you saw outside—but it can be dangerous. Of course, I keep in touch by radio—when the thing works. And I'm pretty self-contained. Last summer they put up a power line—on ordinary poles. What a hope! Blew down in the first storm, just like I told them it would." Bill Roche made no attempt to hide his pleasure at the failure of those feeble toys on which the ordinary, decadent world depends.

"What about supplies?"

"Oh, I stock up. And there used to be a pilot who brought in urgent things. Landed on The Switchback—two miles back down the ridge. He was the only one who'd tackle it. Sometimes he dropped stuff. Once, when the snow was too deep for me to move far, he circled nine or ten times, then dropped a small parachute within ten feet of the front door. Some pilot he was, some pilot. Killed in a glider crash, just last month. Wing fell off. He didn't stand a chance." Bill Roche sat silent for a moment, remembering a man he could respect. Then he stood up. "Well, I'll just go give the animals a last check over for the night."

One of the chemists went with him. When they had gone, the other nodded at the door. "Extraordinary man, Bill Roche," he said. "Perfect for this job. Amazingly self-reliant. Goes out alone in winter to put a track back on a weasel—and those tracks weigh two hundred pounds apiece. Reads a lot too. Quite a pundit on Oriental philosophy, I hear. And he certainly has a way with animals."

"Are all the experiments done with animals?"

"No, about fifty-fifty, animals and people. And Bill's good with people too. Not crabby, like you might expect, living alone at this altitude. We've been up several times, and we always find him easy to get on with."

"What's the exact elevation here?"

"Twelve thousand four hundred and seventy," said the biochemist. "High enough to affect anybody who stays up here for long—and of course there are people who accuse Bill of being a king of his own little castle. Hell, he has to be!"

I nodded. The plateau of White Mountain is no place for a jellyfish.

"He has to put up with some pretty bad weather," went on the biochemist. "Winds up to ninety miles an hour and temperatures around thirty below. Actually, those aren't the worst things. The winter snowstorms are occasionally about as violent as any in the world. Up to five feet in thirty-six hours. He had one like that in December, 1955. And it never gets really warm. Even in summer, fifty-five degrees is about tops. It feels pretty cold to me up here right now—and down in Bishop, at the foot of the mountain, it's been ninety all week."

Bill Roche and the second biochemist came back upstairs. The chemist sank wearily into a chair. "Until you get used to it, this altitude sure hits you," he said. "And not only physically. You can't cogitate up here."

"Cogitate?" said Bill Roche. "Some people get up

here and find they just plain can't think. I've had Ph.D.s who have to go down to Number One Station before they can add two and two."

"Hell!" said one of the biochemists. "Half of us can't do that at sea level."

Bill Roche grinned. "Of course, it affects different people differently. Quite a lot don't seem able to sleep up here at first."

"Maybe not," said the biochemist, levering himself out of the chair. "But right now I feel as if I won't have any difficulty."

Next morning, the biochemists showed me around two big buildings full of caged chickens, rats, rabbits, and guinea pigs. We stopped to give special feed to a group of rabbits.

Suddenly one of the biochemists said, "You think it's wrong, don't you, using them like this? I can see it in your face. But it's all right really, you know. They're quite happy. Look, the door of this cage has been open for five minutes now, and they haven't tried to escape, have they?"

Two big fluffy rabbits—flaccid creatures with mild, almost expressionless eyes—sat in the little cage. The whiskers of one of them brushed the open door. Neither made any attempt to move.

"You see?" said the chemist.

The rabbits were well looked after, of course. They lived contented lives, safe from the hazards their ancestors had faced. Logically, using them experimentally was not only defensible but praiseworthy. A man who works with such animals grows accustomed to their condition—and perhaps he is right. But I found something horrifying about those mild eyes and beautiful, fluffy, flaccid white bodies

—an uncomfortable echo of *Brave New World.* I was glad to get out into the clean, cold world of snow and rock.

The two of us walked back to the Quonset hut. The biochemist had work to do inside. "We'll be staying up here for several days," he said as we shook hands. "You'll probably be off the peak and down in Owens Valley before we are. When you're a plainsman again, remember us up here, won't you?"

"Sure," I promised, half smiling.

It was almost noon before I said good-bye to Bill Roche, out in front of the main building. He nodded northward up the winding jeep road. "Your easiest way is along the road," he said. "It runs clear to the peak. I've cleared most of it, but the last thousand feet of elevation is still blocked by snow. That last stretch, you'd do better to go straight up the slope." He took a key from his pocket. "This'll get you into the summit station. It hasn't been opened this year yet, but there's a butane stove that'll make life easier. And an oil heater too."

He looked up the road toward the ridge that blocked our view of the peak. "You'll like it up on top," he said slowly. "Every time I go, I want to stay there." He sighed. "It's always a struggle to drag myself back down again."

Any worthwhile building reflects its environment; and a building faces problems when it perches on top of a mountain that falls short by only 255 feet of being the highest in the United States.

The summit research station solved its problem by combining the styles of a Maginot Line pillbox and a Riviera villa. It reflected at the same time both the yearlong battle against the elements and also the glorious interludes of sun and spaciousness.

The roof set the pillbox motif. A thick concrete slab, broken only by two lightning conductors and a periscope of a ventilator, sat on the low stone walls with military precision and efficiency. But gay red shutters brought the Riviera to the mountain. When I flung them open they welcomed the sunshine joyfully, as shutters do in Rapallo. (Perhaps I shall be called fanciful for seeing so much in a few painted window screens; but if the shutters were taken down, who would go to Rapallo?)

The station stood on a little tableland, a hundred feet across. On the table itself, the wind was only a wind. But at the rim, even in that calm weather, a deafening gale blew vertically up and away like a jet stream. I presumed the wind had carried up the flies, beetles, and ladybugs that infested the snowdrifts. The summit itself seemed too inhospitable a place to raise such teeming life.

The severity of the summit permeated the research station's interior. Two square rooms housed double-tier bunks, tables and benches, a butane cooking stove, and an oil heater. A wall thermometer registered 37 degrees. On a shelf stood the sign for hanging outside in summer:

WHITE MOUNTAIN RESEARCH
STATION
SUMMIT LABORATORY
ELEVATION 14,246

The temperamental oil heater took the edge off the cold; but it never raised the temperature above 50 degrees at knee level. The cooking stove did better. On it I boiled an egg Bill Roche had given me. ("Laid at 12,470 feet, which is more than most chicks can say.") The water boiled at 84° C. After ten minutes, the egg was still slightly underdone.

I had decided beforehand to test my equipment by sleeping outside. I would not often be able to assemble, at one time and place, a combination of low temperatures, settled weather, and a refuge in case things went wrong.

I was now carrying a small nylon tent that, complete with aluminum poles, weighed 3 pounds 1 ounce. I pitched it in the middle of the plateau on bare stones that had been crushed flat during the station's construction. To protect and insulate the water- and windproof floor, I spread beneath it four sheets of newspaper I had brought up from Bill Roche's kitchen.

Beside the tent, within easy reach, I put the wooden-backed wall thermometer from the laboratory. When I slid into the sleeping bag, swathed in many layers of clothing and with every spare article underneath me, the thermometer registered 27 degrees. With the tent entrance zippered tight, my body soon warmed up and, all in all, I passed a comfortable night. Moments of wakefulness were rare and brief. Of course, it was not a severe test for the equipment. At five o'clock the temperature had not fallen below 25 degrees, and there in the middle of the plateau the wind was mild. But I felt satisfied. With an air mattress or some other good insulation I should have slept as soundly as at home.

At no time during the two days I stayed on the peak was I bitterly cold. But the second night I slept inside. I slept on a top-tier bunk, and I left the heater burning, and that was the only time, as I lay naked in my sleeping bag, that I was warm right through—toes, fingers, marrow, and all.

A view moves forward each day with the same dynamic pattern as the life of an individual or a nation or a species. It is born. It pulses with the vigor of youth. It matures. It dies. Change is its only constant, though the change manifests itself through apparent constants.

Whichever way you look from White Mountain Peak, the view is prefaced by rock and snow. Beyond, you lose yourself in the sweep of immense distance. Eastward, the desert rolls brown and gray and masculine. Westward, the panorama is pink and blue and white and feminine: pink from the floor of Owens Valley, blue from its lakes and from the foothills beyond, white from the spectacle that dominates your mind—the snowcapped facade of the Sierra Nevada.

This is the skeleton of the view. Depth and distance add its sinews.

Owens Valley, though it seems to lie at your feet, is ten thousand feet below. The Sierra snows—so close that you feel you could reach out and grab a handful—are fifty miles away. Northward, the tapering line of peaks never actually ends; instead, at the farthest limit of the horizon, there comes a time when you can at last no longer distinguish snowcap from distant cloud bank.

But the essence of the view—the body and spirit of it—spring from change and progress.

In clear morning sunlight, everything is purity and innocence.

Noon brings deeper knowledge. It sweeps the lingering mist away and reveals unsuspected cracks. Scars and deep ravines appear.

But time softens the disillusion. Evening restores to their proper stature the hills and mountains that afternoon had compressed. At sunset, the Sierra snowcaps are a soft and delicate pink. And then, when it seems this gentleness must end it all, comes the climax.

For a hundred miles across the glowing desert—out beyond the desert itself and up into the haze beyond—there arises, with awesome and inevitable bulk, the vast pyramid of the mountain's shadow. For long, clear-cut minutes it stands as a fitting monument to the day. Then the shadow envelops the whole desert, and it is ready for the night.

The climax is not the end. The view itself sinks into blackness. But a broad double arc of color remains, suspended in the sky around almost a quarter of the horizon. Its lower band is a deep, rich rose; the upper band is palest aquamarine, like the rain-washed sky of an April morning. The arc endures far into the night, fading slowly, almost imperceptibly. It seems possible to hope that it will linger on forever, like the fruitful echoes of a fulfilled life.

I was halfway down the mountain before I glimpsed its strength.

Nothing placates wild country like sunshine; and since that early view of gray clouds swirling about the peak I had lived, day after day, under blue skies. The afternoon I started down the steep western escarpment, the sun still shone; but I underestimated the descent. By sunset I was only halfway down. Soon a rocky pinnacle barred my way. The far slope of the pinnacle was steep and rotten rock. To attempt it in failing light would be to run unnecessary risks. I camped for the night on a narrow ledge.

Before the light finally failed, I looked up. High above, still bright against pale sky, towered the peak. Black ridges soared toward it. I looked down. On every side, ridges plunged into blackness. I felt like a bat clinging halfway up the buttress of a cathedral. There was no question of being afraid. Morning would show me a way out—up if not down. But as I squatted on my ledge, feeling very small, I knew the futility of "ownership." I sensed, as I had never done on the eastern slopes or even on the summit, the power and wildness latent in the huge mass I had presumed to call "my" mountain.

Next morning I climbed down with little difficulty. At ten o'clock I scrambled off the final outcrop onto level sand.

I was a plainsman again.

I remembered to think, as I had promised, of the two biochemists. But not for long. When I looked back up at the crest, far above, I found that daylight had rekindled a half belief in ownership. And when I turned and walked on northward across a flat valley, I was thinking with a sense of loss that I had handed the mountain back to its permanent owners—not only to Bill Roche, safely at home as a good man should be; but to Doug Powell as well, even if he was at that moment being unfaithful with the mountains of Peru.

CHAPTER

7

INTO BODIE

Next to jazz, America's most notable contribution to world lore has so far been The Saga of the Wild West. It is hardly seventy years since The Saga ended, but already its setting has changed beyond recognition. There remain a few isolated and vanishing relics, such as the old frontier I had found along the Colorado. But almost all the towns are gone. In most cases, progress has erased them. A handful have been "preserved" under the varnish of twentieth-century commercialism; but this treatment is only one degree less deadly.

Very few genuine "ghosts" have evaded both physical obliteration and crass commercialism.

The sun had almost set when I came up out of the canyon onto Bodie flat; and by the time I had walked down the mile of dusty road, shadow had fallen over most of the old town.

One shaft of light still slanted through a gap in the hills and cut a swathe through the deserted buildings. For a while it struck life and warmth into their weathered boards and painted deep shadows alongside them. Then it had passed over and left them dark and quiet, and was lighting only the gaunt gray stamp mill on the far slope. Then the mill was quiet too, and it was day only on the scarred hillside above, among the flat-topped mine tailings. Then the sunlight was gone; and everything—the flat and the bare hills and the "ghost" of the town that had changed them—was blue and gray and ready for the night.

I stood for a while on the outskirts of the town, watching the blueness fade and the gray begin to change to black. Then I walked in among the old frame buildings. Most of them stood proud and upright, sagging only a little along the roof ridges. A few leaned tiredly, shored up by old telegraph poles. Some of the windows had been boarded tight; others stared out like empty eye sockets. Among the buildings and along the dusty roads, nothing moved.

I walked on until I found a house with a white sign that said GUARD'S HOME. The guard was a tall, white-haired man who stood with his left side slewed forward so that I could read the inscription on a large silver star: DEPUTY SHERIFF, MONO COUNTY. "Yes, it's quite a place, isn't it?" he said. "Twelve thousand people used to live here once. Back in the seventies, that was. Of course, the town was a whole lot bigger then—before any of the fires. Bodie's always had fires. Last one was after World War II, when they tried to start up again. You can see the burnt-out mill way on top of the hill there, up above the tailings. Bodie took a hundred million dollars' worth of gold from those mines." The guard pointed at the eastern slope where the last sunlight had lingered. In sunshine, the tailings had been many colors: bright sawdust, pale chocolate, sepia, and pure white with green streaks. Now, they had all sunk to a common, neutral buff.

The guard resumed his lecture. "That long gray building down below was Hoover's house . . ."—he waited for me to raise my eyebrows—". . . brother of the president. He lived there with Edison. And over in the museum is the oldest electric motor in the world. We had power in Bodie before 'Frisco did, you know. Yessir, quite a place is Bodie. Oldest unreconstructed 'ghost town' in the nation. Any number of movies been made here.

"Water? Over there, beside those old gas pumps, is the finest water in the Yew-nited States. Piped four and a half miles down from the mountains. But you'll have to camp outside of the town, I'm afraid. No camping in Bodie—and no fires. Well, you'll be wanting to find a place before it gets real dark, but I guess I'll be seeing you tomorrow."

Early next morning I came back into sunlit, empty streets.

The living Bodie must have been an ugly place. The setting is stark: bare, treeless hills surround the treeless flat. The buildings are square and ungainly: although Main Street boasts one or two mildly pretentious facades, the buildings behind them are boxes.

But time has mellowed Bodie. Its few brick buildings have attained a sear and sorrel maturity. Unpainted frame houses, weathered to a deep and resonant brown, dominate every block. Their warmth —which I had thought was "evening glow" —lives on in broad daylight.

Nature has already begun its slow reclamation. Outside a saloon, grass pushes up through cracks in the sidewalk. Sagebrush is closing in on the gray corrugated-iron stamp mill. Wild irises nod in the doorway of a house, half hiding a threshold eroded by many feet.

The echoing past overwhelms the sunlit present. A skewed and gaping fence protects a patch of marsh grass that was once a garden. Wagons that to modern eyes look cumbersome but at the same time spindly still stand on iron-shod wheels; movement, one feels, would destroy them—as air will destroy a body that has lain for centuries in its sealed casket. The buildings, with three or four exceptions, are shells. Floorboards have rotted, and the fussy wallpaper in the more pretentious houses has peeled away. Inside the Methodist church, the wind whistles eerily and stirs up dust among severe, upright pews.

The guard's home, next to the church, was once the banker's house. As I stood and stared at its fine, weathered old front door, I wondered what the city fathers of Bodie would have thought had they known that their booming, rip-roaring town would wither so soon into a tourist curio. And I found myself wondering how long it would be before tourists stood and gaped at the weathered old doors along deserted Wall Street. A place like Bodie has power to jolt our usual myopic human view of time into slightly more realistic focus.

During the morning, a few carloads of tourists trickled into Bodie. I watched one little girl stand on tiptoe and peer through the window of the locked undertaker's shop. Suddenly she turned and ran toward her parents. "Ooooooh!" she cried. "In there, there's father coffins and mother coffins and young coffins too!"

The main tourist center was the museum in the old Miners' Union Hall. Inside, I found the white-haired guard.

"Yes, we're open every day during the tourist season," he said. "Often have quite a crowd up here—a hundred a day, some weekends."

It seemed a meager response to such an opportunity for looking back a hundred years.

"Of course, the road's real bad, and that keeps a lot of folks away. But the money's been appropriated to turn us into a state park. The rangers'll be taking over next year, and they'll put in a hardtop road. Right now, the only income for keeping the place comes from admission fees to this museum. Bodie's still owned by Mr. and Mrs. Cain, you know—both of them born in Bodie. They live down in Bridgeport now. Mrs. Cain wrote this book about the history of the town and it's turned into quite a best-seller." The guard picked a brown softcover book from the top of a pile. "I'm just going off to lunch, but you can sit here and read if you like. My wife'll be looking after the museum the rest of the day."

So I sat down in a corner of Bodie Miners' Union Hall and opened *The Story of Bodie* by Ella M. Cain.

The evening before, as I watched the sunlight cut a swathe across the old town, my usually inert historical imagination had twitched. All morning, as I wandered through the sunlit streets, it had been stirring. Mrs. Cain's book brought it leaping to its feet.

The book is no literary masterpiece. But Mrs. Cain has not written history; she has written a story she watched unfold. Even the anecdotes she retails are those she often heard in childhood.

Mrs. Cain was born in a house that still stands opposite the Methodist church. William Bodey had struck gold on that inhospitable flat in 1859, more than twenty years earlier; but until 1877 the town that was misspelled after him never registered more than twenty voters. The boom came in 1878. News of rich strikes echoed around the gold-hungry West. Men poured in. They came from San Francisco, from declining Virginia City, from the Mother Lode. The highways were jammed with twenty-mule teams, dead-axle wagons, and pack trains. Prospectors trudged along beside laden burros. The Bodie stage line, using fifty-four horses, ran eight regular stages. Within a year, shares in Bodie Mining Company rocketed from fifty cents to fifty-four dollars and the town's population from a handful to ten or twelve thousand.

Mrs. Cain was born three years later.

From the beginning, Bodie's badness outshone even its fabulous wealth. A popular morning greeting among miners was, "Have we a man for breakfast?" A free-shooting character known as "Two Gun Al" maintained that he doubled up because he "didn't want to feel naked in Bodie." Murder cases often started in the opium dens of Chinatown; but the most famous began in the Miners' Union Hall in which I was reading.

During a dance, a Frenchman paid undue attention to the wife of a mild-mannered Cornishman. The Frenchman suggested they go outside to talk things over. Sixty paces down the street he put a gun to the unarmed Cornishman's head and pulled the trigger. The man dropped in the snow, a bleeding corpse.

There was talk of a lynching. As protection against

the mob, the prisoner was removed from jail and placed under special guard in a lodging house. That night, "presumably while the guard slept," he escaped. The outraged citizens formed a Vigilante Committee. They recaptured the Frenchman, brought him back to Bodie, and manhandled a huge wagon crane to the place the Cornishman's blood still stained the snow. At midnight, a noose was placed around the prisoner's neck and twenty men took hold of the rope and walked slowly away. The body rose, twisting and writhing. The Justice of the Peace entered in his records: "Case dismissed, as the defendant was taken out and hanged by a mob."

The Vigilante Committee afterward ran so many undesirable characters out of town that, all over the West, anyone who admitted he had been near the place was taunted with the stock question, "Are you the Bad Man from Bodie?"

The town's reputation grew. One distant newspaper editor printed the prayer of a little girl: "Goodbye God! I'm going to Bodie." The editor of Bodie's paper claimed the girl had been misquoted. What she had actually said was: "Good, by God! I'm going to Bodie."

Life in Bodie was lived by warm-blooded men and women—unpolished perhaps, but crackling with vitality. Mrs. Cain's book keeps bursting out with stories no one could invent.

It tells of the undying rivalry between the two butchers' wives—the snobbish Englishwoman and the attractive ex-prostitute. It traces the corruption of the young Indian girl who became mistress of Chinatown's Tong boss, took to opium, and finally killed herself by eating handfuls of poison parsnip.

There was "Lying Jim" Townsend—friend of Bret

Harte and Mark Twain, and editor of one of Bodie's papers—maintaining that "all you need to make a good mine is a hole in the ground and a good liar."

There was honest Hank Blanchard, tollhouse keeper and graduate of an Ivy League college, reacting to a suggestion that he go "on the wagon" with: "I've given up my home, my family, my money, and my self-respect for drink—now why should I give up drink?"

There was old Buffalo Bill with his "hound dog" who helped him thieve anything he could lay hands on. One winter, neighbors found suspicious marks in the snow around their woodpiles. One of them packed a hollowed log with "giant powder" and planted it on top of a pile. A few days later the front of Buffalo Bill's shack blew out and he found himself sitting outside in the snow, so black that even his old hound dog hardly knew him.

And always there were fires—from the disaster of 1892 that gutted Bodie's mile-long Main Street to the blaze of 1932 that finally closed the town down. A sidelight on one of the fires brought home to me the authenticity of Mrs. Cain's book. She describes two granddaughters of the town banker standing across the street from the bank while it burned to the ground. One of the girls clutched a Webster's dictionary. The other held the skeleton of a horned toad she had rescued from a display cabinet. It is easy to picture the skeleton standing in the girls' home for many years and to hear the story being told and retold. The girls—though the book does not say so—were Mrs. Cain's daughters.

When I at last dragged myself away from *The Story of Bodie* and walked around the museum, the words took solid shape. Ranged about the excellent dancing floor on which the Frenchman had flirted with the Cornishman's wife were the last relics of living Bodie: oversize snowshoes for the horses (Bodie, at 8,300 feet, sometimes winters under nine or ten feet of snow); pictures of Chinatown in the '80s; a grocer's ledger with an entry for August 1879 listing—in the superb flowing hand that was then a prime requirement for bookkeeping:

	$	¢
2# butter	—	65
23# bacon	4	60
581# potatoes	29	05
2 Galls brandy	9	—;

the wrought-iron red light that Rosa May, one of the more famous ladies of Bodie's red-light district, brought from her native Paris and hung above her door in Maiden Lane (or was it around the corner in Virgin Alley?); and—linking history to the flesh-and-blood present—a group photograph of the self-conscious young men who made up the "Bodie Mutts" baseball team of 1907–8.

The guard's wife showed me several copies of *The Miner Index*, the paper "Lying Jim" Townsend had edited. The "squib" column for January 1, 1898, reflected his major interests—debtors, politicians, the badness of Bodie, and the town's feud with the "rival" centers of San Francisco and Los Angeles:

> Happy New Year to all who have paid the printer.
>
> William Jennings Bryan has been discharging his mouth so vigorously in Mexico that several volcanoes have broken out.

> Judge Wallace having dismissed the contempt proceedings against Juror Smythe, it looks as though Durrant will on the 7th pass to Sheol with the mark of a hemp tie around his neck.
>
> For a city of its size and commercial advantages, San Francisco is the slowest place in the world. There is but one tolerable street in the place, though there are more than 11,000 empty buildings. A great proportion of the people who surge through the dilapidated thoroughfares are homeless and hungry. The town is on the wrong side of the bay. If the citizens of Oakland would pull together for a few years, the Bay City would be a very bad second in the race.
>
> To read the Los Angeles papers and swallow unreservedly their self-adulation, one would conclude that there is no other place in the universe. Even Boston and Heaven are ignored.

"Lying Jim" sometimes peered into a clouded crystal ball. I was able to mail the *San Francisco Chronicle*, for whom I was writing weekly articles, an early view of its sole present-day competitor:

> The Examiner proposes to start an evening paper about the first of the New Year. If young Mr. Hearst don't watch out he'll go broke on some of his schemes. San Francisco already has more newspapers than it can properly support. They are too big and bladdery.

By the time I tore myself away from the museum it was late afternoon. I walked past the Methodist church, past the frame house in which Mrs. Cain was born, and climbed up the gentle slope to the cemetery.

The living Bodie was rigidly divided into three sectors: the respectable quarter, Chinatown, and the red-light district. Death lifted no barriers. Only people of impeccable character—impeccable by Bodie's standards—were buried inside the fence of the "respectable" cemetery. In doubtful cases, the town sat in judgment on the deceased to decide whether their sins merited relegation to that unhallowed area below the fence known as "Boot Hill"—named for, but not restricted to, those who died with their boots on. Tempers sometimes ran so high at judgment meetings that guns helped decide the verdict and the cemetery received more than its scheduled quota.

All Chinese were buried *above* the fence. Today, almost nothing is left of their cemetery: the bones were long ago exhumed and shipped back to China. But this little annex to the cemetery was once a magnet for hungry Piute Indians who had learned that quantities of food, including traditional roast pork, were always placed on new Chinese graves.

"Boot Hill," too, is now little but a sagebrush slope. Markers were rarely raised here. Even the once carefully tended grave of Rosa May of Maiden Lane is now a pathetic, leaning little square of picket fence. There is nothing to mark the resting place of many others—of James DaRoche, the Frenchman strung up at midnight above the blood of his victim; of Neva Pine, who died from an overdose of opium; of Charlie Jardine, shot through the heart by "Pioche" Kelley; of Jim Desmond, who died with his boots on in a saloon row; of "Peek-a-boo" Patten, a sporting woman; or of Henry Chatterton, who died of exposure while drunk.

The respectable cemetery is Bodie's leading tourist draw, but it is even less of a spectacle than most cemeteries. The stock-in-trade of faded sorrow is accentuated by neglect. Tourist feet keep the sagebrush at bay, but few graves are maintained. The most imposing monument, a tall granite shaft, bears the rather surprising inscription:

ERECTED
TO
THE MEMORY
OF
JAMES A. GARFIELD

This shaft commemorates the fickleness of men. In 1879, with Bodie booming, the population subscribed five hundred dollars for a monument to mark the new resting place of its founder, William Bodey. (Bodey had perished in a snowstorm, close to camp, a few months after making his strike. Not until 1879, twenty years later, were his bones and bowie knife and pistol rediscovered where they had been buried next spring by his partner. The partner was himself murdered soon afterward by Piute Indians at the foot of White Mountain after a fight in which he left ten attackers dead on the floor of his cabin. The fate of the two prospectors bore out the mining superstition that discovers of worthwhile camps die tragic deaths.) The granite monument to William Bodey was completed in 1881, just as news of President Garfield's assassination reached Bodie. Sentiment ran so high that the citizens reallocated the monument. Today it is the focal point of Bodie cemetery—while the bones of the town's founder lie somewhere nearby in an unmarked grave.

Also nearby is a gray headstone with a curious hole in the center. This grave lifts the cemetery out of history and into the present—or at least into yesterday. Two brass plates used to enclose the hole. During Prohibition, when Bodie was at its last gasp, the local bootlegger would remove one plate under cover of darkness and cache his bottles of liquor in the hole. When the saloonkeeper accepted delivery, he deposited money in the same place.

The bare cemetery hillside commands a panoramic view of Bodie. Looking down from it, I saw the town for the first time as an isolated outpost in a hostile setting. I could picture miners coming off shift in temperatures of 40 below—the "real pneumonia weather" that Mrs. Cain remembered. I could imagine ten feet of snow filling Main Street, and tunnels being dug from one sidewalk to the other. I could feel the cold biting into William Bodey as he stumbled his last steps.

A cool evening breeze blew off the hills behind me, and I started down the hill.

As I walked, I wondered if there were other "ghost towns" as unspoiled and evocative. And I wondered what it was about Bodie that had caught my imagination. But perhaps, I thought, not everyone would sense a past-come-alive in the brown skeletons of Bodie's houses. Perhaps I would not always do so myself: our appreciation of ghosts, as of everything, depends very much on our mood of the moment.

Perhaps it was just that when I came over the hill and saw Bodie for the first time my mood was ripe.

And yet I do not think so. The mood persisted, undiminished, for twenty-four hours. Exactly twenty-four hours.

By the time I was ready to leave Bodie, the not-quite-melancholy warmth of evening sunlight was again spreading over warped wooden walls, deepening the resonant brown that had for me become the town's signature. A fitful wind whined in old power lines. The last tourist had gone and the guard had driven away on some errand.

I was glad to be alone with Bodie and its ghosts as I walked out over the flat. I passed the faint oval that had been the racecourse and turned south. Beside the hill that would block my last view of the town, I stopped and looked back.

The shaft of light was once more slanting through the western hills onto the pattern of brown walls. Among the farthest buildings, the gray and blue of night was winning its daily victory. As I watched, the shadows began to creep forward and reach up for the stamp mill and the scarred hillside beyond.

Beyond Bodie I walked for forty miles toward the snow peaks of the Sierra Nevada. As I went, I watched the country shade from semi-desert into green and pleasant foothills.

At first I walked through country as barren as Bodie was flat. Sagebrush scratched at my bare legs. Cicadas rasped in the sunshine. Blue-haloed grasshoppers clapper-rattled on short, clumsy flights.

Then the creeks began. And with them came richer animal life. Coiled blue water snails roosted on the bed of a source spring. Silvery fish, big as herrings, patrolled its cress beds.

The creeks began to support meadows—coarse and marshy at first, then svelte with cropped turf. The sagebrush receded. My legs rediscovered nettles. A patch of shallow water supported half a dozen ducks and thirty inexplicable sea gulls. Imprinted on a patch of wet mud I saw my first raccoon tracks since Mexico. Soon, out in the open, there were three does browsing.

At lunchtime on the second day I stepped down onto a grassy creek bank and routed an amphibious division of small frogs—olive-backed, white-bellied, and yellow-warted—that dove in frenzy and *en bloc* into the water and swam away on the surface, forelegs held close to their bodies.

By the third day I was walking through knee-deep meadow grass. On the meadow's flanks, aspens whispered mountain secrets. And late on the third afternoon I came at last to the West Walker River. It was a full-scale, jostling trout stream. Pine trees lined its banks. A rough-hewn board said PICNIC AREA. Out in a meadow, sunlight flashed from the rods of red-shirted fishermen. Above them—close now, and inviting—towered Sierra peaks.

My imagination leaped up to the crest. Beyond it waited a new and different sample of America. And it was more than the mountains themselves that I was thinking of. Every genuine fishing addict is inclined, illogical as it may be, to let his view of a country be colored by the kind of fishing he finds there. From what I had heard, the fishing beyond that crest—in the valley of the Silver King—promised to be something special. All through the desert I had been curbing daydreams of it: as a killer of pleasure there is nothing to compare with over-anticipation. But now at last I could give events their head.

CHAPTER

8

BESIDE THE SILVER KING

An addiction to fishing can do many things for a man, but none of them quite compares with the way it can, very occasionally, defeat the clock.

A boy of six or eight or thirteen starts every new day expecting a miracle or two to happen before sunset. Put a fishing rod in his hand, and expectation edges toward certainty. In bright morning sunlight he hurries down the familiar trail that leads to the river. As he goes, he saves precious fishing time by gulping down his sandwich lunch. He reaches the river—and the whole, wide, exciting world narrows down to that first, still-uncaught fish.

In due time the boy becomes the man. He may, unfortunately, atrophy into a grim-faced fish slayer. But if he grows up he finds that the catching of fish comes to matter less and less. He savors subtler joys—joys that he refuses to examine too closely for fear analysis will shatter them. But he knows, though he rarely admits it even to himself, that somehow, somewhere along the line, he has lost something.

The years pass. Then chance provides the right

company or the right solitude, the right elation or the right despair, the right sunlight or the right rain. And to these is added, at the right time and place, some new and piquant element. It trips a tumbler. Something the man had almost forgotten wells up inside him; for a brief interlude he recaptures his youth.

Such interludes are very rare. But the man remembers them for the rest of his life.

During the month of hectic planning back in San Francisco, I had spoken on the phone one day to a friend named Herb Pintler in the California Fish and Game Department.

"Guess you'll be going through Alpine Country," he said. "I know a place up there just made for you. Wild country it is, almost untouched. And a little creek called Silver King with special cutthroat trout that not many people know about. Isolated variants they are, quite different from ordinary cutthroats. Beautiful little fish. Would you like some literature on them?"

"Surely," I said. "I doubt if I'll be able to spend any time there but . . ."

Herb had laughed quietly into the phone. "Once you get up there," he said, "you'll *make* time."

Even then, before I knew any more, I think I felt something stir inside me. And when, high above the West Walker River, I climbed the final snowbank into a ten-thousand-foot pass, I knew at last what I had heard in Herb Pintler's voice. Beyond the snowbank, the mountainside dropped away again. And there below me lay the valley of the Silver King.

Timbered slopes plunged down a twisting V that

held the creek. Two miles downstream, a meadow showed emerald green. Beyond, peak after Sierra peak stretched away northward to the horizon. There was no sign that man's hand had touched a single leaf or a single blade of grass.

As I dug my staff in the snow to ease the weight of the pack, I knew for certain what I had suspected all along: that I was going to find much more in the Silver King than a special kind of trout. Already I could feel the valley's fascination. Deep shadow covered its far slopes. From the shadow, treetops thrust up like green stalagmites into slanting sunshine. The contrast and interplay between sunlight and shadow gave the place a leprechaun air of almost-too-perfect enchantment.

After a while I began to walk down the mountainside. The snow ended. Trees began again. Among the pines and firs, giant junipers appeared, the spiraling bark of their orange trunks reaching up sixty feet and more. A doe stared at me from the far side of a clearing, uncertain whether to be frightened. A bar of sunlight, piercing the forest shadow, floodlit a crimson columbine. Then I reached the first shrill waters of the creek and walked through beds of sunflowers and lupines and scarlet Indian paintbrush.

By the time I pitched camp, the creek had matured. Its pools had taken on that depth—a certain depth of color rather than any linear measure—that every trout fisherman knows means fish. But somehow the urge to fish did not come. I did not mind though: I knew the fish would wait. For I knew that this beautiful little valley had been kept hidden away in secrecy for no one but me. And the knowledge was no less exciting because the grown-up, down-to-earth part of me knew that it was complete nonsense.

Next morning I began fishing before breakfast. I knew exactly what I was looking for. Back in San Francisco I had carefully studied the Fish and Game Department literature Herb Pintler had sent. It began with the usual prosaic ichthyologists' stuff: In the headwaters of Silver King Creek existed a distinct subspecies of Lahontan cutthroat or black-spotted trout. This isolated variant, called Piute trout after the local Indians, was readily recognizable by the absence of spots on the body, by parr marks carried throughout life, and, above all, by its purple coloration. It was long ago segregated from the original stock by the barrier of Llewellyn Falls, and down the centuries had developed its own distinctive pattern of coloration.

But as I read on I realized that the fish must be more than just a scientific oddity. Even the ichthyologists got carried away. They talked of "an iridescent sheen like the play of colors in a Mexican fire opal." And they named the fish Seleniris—after Selene, Greek goddess of the moon—because of "a fancied resemblance of its evanescent tints to the lunar rainbow."

So that first morning beside the Silver King I knew exactly what I was looking for.

I caught no fish before breakfast. Fishing is like that, I told myself. If it were not, money spent on fishing licenses would be better invested in fish markets. But by lunchtime I had still caught nothing. Late in the afternoon I shouldered my pack and began to work down the valley, fishing as I went. By seven o'clock I had still seen no sign of a fish.

And then, below a steep cascade, I came to a line of beaver ponds. Around them, gnawed aspen stumps gleamed white, like broken pencil points.

As I pushed through the aspens bordering the second pond, I stopped in my tracks. A side creek fed the pond. And above its gravel bed, suspended in less than a foot of water, hung a shape that was not quite motionless. A shaft of sunlight, slanting through the trees, glistened on tints and hues I had never before seen in a trout.

My breath suddenly short, I eased down out of sight and slipped off the pack. As I crept downstream, the little fly rod quivered in my shaking hand. Three or four yards, and I lifted my head. The fish still hung suspended above the gravel. It was no more than nine inches long—but that did not matter. What mattered was the subtle lavender sheen glistening in the sunlight.

When I lifted the rod to cast, I could feel my heart pounding as if it wanted to break loose. And it was then, with my breath coming fast and shallow and the rod shaking like an aspen in my hand, that I realized what had happened. A little nine-inch fish had stripped away the cocoon of mature indifference and flicked my calendar back almost thirty years. I was the boy of six or eight or thirteen, waiting for a miracle. The whole wide, exciting world had narrowed down to that first, still-uncaught fish.

My excitement wrecked the first cast. The fly curled out too far, rapped against a tree—and snagged. I lowered the rod, pulled directly on the line, and prayed. The thin nylon leader broke at the fly and catapulted back to me. The trout still hovered in mid-water, undisturbed.

I unclipped another fly from my fly box and with

fumbling fingers tied it to the leader. On the second cast, the fly flicked neatly under a beaver-felled sapling and landed just upstream of the trout. It sank and swept down over the gravel. The trout eased to one side, opened its mouth, and moved back into place. I tightened.

The fish rushed upstream, felt the power of the rod, turned, and headed back down toward a submerged log. For a moment I just held on, the rod kicking in my hand. Then the fish turned again, and I knew I had won. Seconds later I was kneeling and staring at its quivering scales.

Even as I broke its neck and put it out of pain, my eyes took in the details of its markings. But the details faded before the discovery of what had moved the ichthyologists to poetry. Out of the water, the trout's lavender sheen was brilliant purple, underlaid with a golden flush that at the head flamed almost to red. And all of these colors were subtle and changing. The ichthyologists' "iridescent sheen" and "evanescent tints" were no poetic fancies.

In the next twenty minutes I learned as well why the ichthyologists had reported "tints and shades that come and go with every changing whim of the fish." In that twenty minutes I caught three more Piutes. Each of them had under its lower jaw the thin scarlet slashes that give cutthroat trout their name; and each had along its flanks the parr marks that most trout lose at maturity—a regular series of black smudges like a full set of fingerprints. But their coloring varied from pale lavender to a deep, royal purple.

The fourth fish was a little bigger than the others, about eleven inches. The moment it was hooked it jumped high in the evening sunlight, cartwheeling toward me; soon another Piute was staging a war dance on the bank. As I knelt beside it, staring in wonder at the colors that came and went on its quivering scales, I understood why Herb Pintler had said I would *make* time to stay beside the Silver King. Already I was determined to know more about these little trout. I wanted to find out for myself how large they grew and how much their tantalizing colors varied. I wanted to discover the feeding places they liked best—fast water or slow, pools or shallow runs, the main current or the back eddies. I wanted to know what flies they would take, and how they fought—and tasted. And, almost more than anything else, I wanted to see a hybrid.

Herb Pintler had mentioned hybrids that day on the phone, back in San Francisco. "I've never seen one myself," he said. "But you'll maybe run into one or two. Way back, a few rainbows and ordinary cutthroats were planted above Llewellyn Falls, and Piutes are supposed to have crossed with both. If you do catch a hybrid, I'd certainly appreciate seeing some transparencies."

In spite of their color variations, I felt fairly sure that none of the fish I'd caught had been hybrids. And already, for no very clear reason, I had made up my mind to catch one. I would like some color slides for Herb Pintler; but that was only an excuse. I just knew, the way you do about some things, that I would not be happy until I had succeeded.

As I walked on downstream, beginning to look for a campsite that would do for more than one day, I could almost hear Herb Pintler saying, "I told you so."

The faint trail I followed was lined with aspens. Carved into the bark of some of them were names and dates, blackened with age. FELIX LARRANETA, 1914, said one. MIGUEL YIURRALDE, JUUO 27, 1912, said another. Names carved on trees usually disgust me. But these blackened letters had a quiet and unexpected dignity. Perhaps it was just their age. But it was partly, I think, because I knew they had been carved by Basque sheepherders, the same hardy breed as the Frenchmen who had penetrated with their sheep to the inaccessible plateau near White Mountain Peak. I found myself hoping I would meet one of them—or one of their sons or grandsons.

I walked on downstream. A blue jay catcalled from a juniper branch. A subcommittee of gophers inspected me, pious paws together, before retiring for debate. A furry marmot peered around a tree stump, the black bar across his nose quivering indecisively as doubt fought a visible battle with curiosity.

By the time I found a good camp I was wishing I could spend a month in this secret, strangely unreal valley. It was not only the trout. I wanted as well to explore its quiet forest, its sunlit meadows, and the snow-covered peaks that towered above them.

In the end, I "made time," as Herb Pintler had put it, to spend a week beside the Silver King.

For three days I did not move outside the little meadow I had camped in. Close up, it still had the leprechaun enchantment, almost too good to be true, that I had felt up at the pass.

The first morning, I woke as the sun broke clear of the forest. Out in the dew-covered meadow a buck was browsing, its outline luminous against silver and sunlight. Suddenly it raised its antlered head. Its body tensed. Unhurriedly, but without hesitation, it trotted to the edge of the forest. For a moment it stood there, alert. Then it had faded into the shadows.

In my little meadow I found something to suit every kind of fly-fisherman.

At its head were the beaver ponds, tailor-made for the man with enough control of his casting to keep the fly out of standing trees and with enough sense of balance to work his way along felled ones. Down the middle of the meadow, the creek meandered in a chain of pools and runs. You had to crouch far back from the open bank and drop your fly onto a target the size of a small frying pan. At the foot of the meadow, where the trees drew in again, the creek plunged headlong over granite boulders, then lingered between them in rocky pools. Here was Polaroid-and-infantry fishing, that I rate the best kind of fishing in the world: Polaroid sunglasses to penetrate surface glare and show you the fish; and an infantry training to get you close enough, by every device of creeping and crawling and slow movement and simple camouflage, to drop a fly precisely where the fish will find it hardest to resist.

My meadow had more than fishing too. It was a place of ever-changing moods. Each morning I woke to sunshine. But in late afternoon clouds built up, black as bears, and blocked out the sun. Often they drifted away northward, unfulfilled. But sometimes rain or hail lashed down like a whip. Lightning jabbed among the peaks and thunder crashed down into the somber valley. Half an hour, and rainbows were curving out over the glistening trees. At the edge of the beaver ponds, the filigree branches of dead firs glowed with a strange, diffused mauve that was not quite of this world. And in the morning the valley was once more vivid with sunlight.

Sunshine, rain, or hail, the little Piute trout went on taking my flies. They might have been fasting for a week, just waiting for me to arrive. I got used to seeing the creek's surface punctured by the pink cheeks of rising fish. And as the days passed I pieced together what I had made up my mind to discover about Piutes.

I learned that they lived in all parts of the river; that they took almost any kind of fly—"wet" (sinking) or "dry" (floating); that they did not seem to grow longer than eleven inches; that they always fought strongly but rarely spectacularly; and that they tasted like . . . well, like trout.

It is no use asking whether they tasted better than other trout. When you're cooking outdoors and the fish are so fresh that it is a problem to stop them curving into loops in the frying pan, you don't bother your head about comparisons. All you are conscious of is hunger. You taste the smallest fish to check it if is ready. And you go on taking mouthfuls until it is finished. By that time the others are ready. So you take the pan off the fire and put in on a flat stone and devour every one of those crisp-skinned little fish without pausing—direct from the pan, piping hot, and dripping with butter. All you can say when you've finished is that trout are the most perfect food man ever tasted. The Piutes tasted like that.

I learned, too, how right the ichthyologists had been about "changing tints." One fish was abnormally pale when I landed it. I reached for my camera. Inside thirty seconds I had focused; but already the fish was the normal Piute purple. Most dead fish darkened to a deep coppery purple, almost black. A few kept their original shade. Others faded to tarnished silver, almost white, with a pale orange band along each flank.

But after three days in the meadow, in spite of everything I had learned about Piutes, I had still not caught a hybrid.

The most likely place to catch one seemed to be just above or below Llewellyn Falls, the barrier that for centuries had cut Piutes off from the trout below. And on the fourth afternoon I moved down toward the falls.

On the way I met the only four people I saw all week.

First there were two Forest Rangers on horseback who said they only got up that far about once a year.

Later, when I reached a stout log cabin that the map called "Connell's Cow Camp," two characters who might have stepped out of a western movie were hitching their horses to a rail.

One of them was an oak of a man with a face like a good-humored walnut. "Howdy!" he said, keeping to the script. "My name's Charlie Roberts. And this is Sid Henderson."

Sid Henderson, lean and amiable, grinned at me from under a new straw hat that almost swamped him.

Charlie Roberts looked up at the threatening afternoon sky. "Likely going to rain any minute," he said. "You'd best come on in out of it. Come to that, why not stop over with us tonight? Plenty of bunks in the cabin."

It is always difficult to say no to a man like Charlie Roberts. When he suggests something that has already begun to form in your mind, refusal becomes comfortably impossible.

Sid Henderson hung up his straw hat in the cabin, handling it as a woman would a Dior creation, then went out to unsaddle the horses.

Charlie cleaned out a massive iron stove. As he worked, he told me he ranched down to the east of the mountains on the edge of the Nevada desert. "But I was born in West Texas," he said with pride. "Sid now, he's a Californian. Good man too. One of the best horsemen I've got."

The storm broke directly overhead. For ten minutes, torrential rain lashed down. Then the clouds broke up and retreated.

Sid went to the door and looked out across the glistening meadow. "How's about a mess o' trout tonight, Charlie? . . . OK, I'll go dig a few worms."

Five minutes later we were walking together across the meadow. Sid jerked his worm tin back toward the cabin. "Quite a man, that Charlie. Owns half a dozen ranches down in Nevada—God knows how many acres altogether. Worth a load o' money—and very conservative with it; but if it comes to a pinch he'll give you the shirt off his back. You couldn't find a better man to work for."

Near the cabin, the creek was swift and turbulent—a better place for fishing with worms than with flies. In half an hour I squeezed out four mediocre fish with my flies. Sid Henderson, parading along the open bank with no attempt to conceal himself or his hat, hauled out ten good ones on worms. But still there was no hybrid among them.

Supper looked like the feeding of five thousand. "Seven summers I've been coming up here now," said Charlie as he ladled onto his plate three trout and three separate mounds of macaroni, onions, and fried potatoes. "Two or three days every month, June through September. And one thing I always look forward to is a mess o' trout. Mind you, there's other things too. I can understand what old man Connell liked about this place—he's the guy that built the first cabin here. Fifty-nine summers he'd been coming up. He'd set his heart on making it sixty straight, but he got some kind of heart trouble and his wife talked him out of it. He died three years back." Charlie shook his head. "Seems a pity, doesn't it? If he made it sixty he'd have been happy . . . and, hell, we're all going to die sometime.

"Sixty years . . . Quite a spell. And I guess this place hasn't changed much. Seems to me like there used to be more bears though. I remember one stripping a dead cow once. Nothing but bones left next day. But it must be two years now since I saw a bear."

I asked about some mud holes I had seen out in the meadow.

"Warm water, all of 'em," said Charlie. "And an old Piute Indian I knew said there's minerals in 'em too. I ought to have somebody come up and check —it's a thing I've been laying off to do for quite a while now."

"Are the Piutes a good crowd?" I asked.

Charlie wiped his mouth with the back of a massive hand. "Guess they're like Indians anyplace," he said. "Same as down in West Texas. Much the same as white men. Some of them's damned fine fellows, and some of them ain't worth a damn."

Soon after supper we went to bed.

"You know," said Charlie as he put out the lamp.

"I think this is the first time I've found anybody else up here. I hear tell a few hunters come up in the fall, but I always have the cattle out by then. Don't trust those hunters. Aside from them, I guess there's never been too many people up this far. They logged some, back in the seventies, though. Mostly tamaracks."

"Tamaracks?"

"Lodgepole pines. Tamaracks, we call 'em around here. Chinamen logged 'em off in winter for mines down on the Comstock Lode—Virginia City and the like. This is about as high as they came though."

"Chinamen?" I said. "I didn't know they did any logging."

"Neither did I. But I've always been told it was Chinamen. There used to be cabins all down the creeks. There's still one with the roof left on, and another where they shot their oxen . . ."

"Shot their oxen? What for?"

"*Shod*," said Charlie, "*Shod* them. Blacksmith's shop. You can still see the old anvil. They used oxen to haul logs over the snow to the river, and they built dams to hold the water back. You can still see what's left of some of the dams. When the big thaw came they'd let the dams go and float the logs clear down into Nevada."

I lay for some time in the darkened cabin, trying to picture Chinese loggers up in that country. Somehow I couldn't quite bring the picture into focus.

Sid's voice, coming from the other side of the cabin, broke my line of thought. "Before you came up into the mountains," he said, "did you go 'round by Mono Lake?"

I had skirted just east of the lake, where people

had said I would find volcanic craters; but the country turned out to be about as volcanic as Long Island. It had certainly been quiet though. On the Fourth of July I had walked twenty miles along a public road and seen nobody at all. "And I doubt if there are too many places in the United States you can still do that," I said. "But it was the one really dull stretch of California I've come through. Nothing but sand and sage and juniper."

"I know what you mean," said Charlie out of the darkness. "But that Mono's quite a lake, all the same. Alkali—strong alkali. If you want to wash a set of dirty clothes, all you have to do is put them on and jump into that water and take a swim. Or so they say."

"Yeah," said Sid. "Even if they're greasy from working on your automobile, that'll clean 'em up. But if you leave 'em in the lake all night, maybe you'll find nothing there in the morning."

There was silence while Charlie digested this information. Then: "I'll tell you one thing," he said. "If you jump into that lake with your hair dyed, the dye'll be gone inside of two or three minutes."

The silence was longer this time. A coyote yowled in the distance. I looked away from the open window, where tree tracery still showed against pale sky, and turned my face to the wall.

"I've heard tell," said Sid, "that if you use the water from the lake on a horse's back for a couple of days, it'll clear up soreback."

The top tier of the bunk shielded me from such faint light as still came through the window. Against the wall it was pitch black. The silence lengthened into night.

I was almost asleep when Charlie spoke again.

"I'll tell you one thing," he murmured, half to himself it seemed. "People do funny things. Humans, anyway."

Two days later—it was the sixth day since I had come over the pass—Charlie and Sid rode back down out of the mountains into Nevada, and I went back to my hunt for a hybrid Piute.

I tried first below Llewellyn Falls, the staircase of raging white water that had created the Piutes as a subspecies and still presumably marked their lower limit. It seemed likely that a few fish would have been swept down and interbred with other trout. But in four hours' hard fishing I caught only rainbow trout; not one Piute, let alone a hybrid.

I climbed back above Llewellyn Falls, into Piute country again. Within sound of the falls, a grassy basin nestled among bare rocks. The creek swirled through its neck, then widened into a deep pool. Halfway down the pool, where the water died into flatness, a trout sucked down a surface insect.

I flicked out a small dry fly. It floated downstream, glistening in the sunlight. Then a dark nose broke the surface. The fly disappeared. I tightened—and the fly came back without the hook even pricking. I cast again, and this time the fish slashed wildly, showing silvery scales and gill plates. And then I woke up. Piutes were never silvery; and their gill plates always showed pink. In Piute country that could only mean one thing.

And all at once, for the second time in a week, the years were stripped away. The wide, exciting world once more narrowed down to a single, still-uncaught fish.

With trembling schoolboy fingers I dried the fly and fluffed out its hackle feather. Then I cast again, up near the head of the pool. The fly bounced attractively down. I held my breath. The fly passed the crucial spot. I began to let my breath go. Then the fish slashed again, silvery and furious. I counted three, then struck. The rod arched.

Moments later I was kneeling in the grass beside a slender, silvery trout. Measured by my excitement, it might have been ten pounds instead of ten inches. The fish had no Piute purple and no parr marks; just black spots on its silvery sides and white belly. And I had to peer close to see the faint pink cutthroat slash under each jaw. I didn't know just what the fish was, but it certainly wasn't a straight cutthroat. Up in Piute country, it had to be a hybrid.

I took several color shots for Herb Pintler. And then, as I closed the camera, I saw that with success I had lost my last excuse for lingering beside the Silver King.

Slowly I packed away my tackle. I took a long, final look at the snow peaks dominating the head of the valley. Then I heaved the pack onto my back and headed down the trail. Within a quarter mile, trees deadened the roar of the falls. I walked on, feeling as if I had lost something. But the valley's leprechaun enchantment, its too-good-to-be-true unreality, came with me. It was still there when I camped that night in a meadow ten miles below Llewellyn Falls. It was still there next morning when I walked through an aspen grove with more Basque names carved into the silvery trunks. Again I found myself hoping I would meet some of these hardy sheepherders. One of them, a sentimentalist named SIMONUEVO OTRANNO, feeling as I did now, had carved beneath his name ADIOS SIERRA. I walked on down the valley, trying to forget the "adios," trying to remember that a hundred miles of High Sierra still lay ahead.

The enchantment was still there when the Silver King lost its identity at last in a bigger stream. Man had still not touched a single leaf. Then, a mile below the junction, I came to a road. It was only a narrow, tortuous, boulder-strewn kind of a jeep road; but it was enough. It meant vehicles and post offices and progress. It meant that, whether I liked it or not, I had come back to the fringes of the dull, adult, workaday, non-leprechaun world.

Alpine County (in which Silver King Creek both rises and falls) has a past of which it is proud and a population that is the smallest of any county in the United States. And all conversation in Alpine County, given time, gravitates toward these twin topics like a compass needle toward the north.

Failing conversation, a glance at a map will suggest the outline of Alpine's history. Silver King Creek, Silver Peak, and Silver Mountain City disclose that there was once a mining boom in this remote backwater of California. Jeff Davis Peak, Pickett's Peak, and Fredericksburg date the boom, for most of the men who swarmed into Alpine in the late 1860s were Civil War veterans. And Fremont Peak, Carson River, and the Carson Range hint at Alpine's share in The Saga of the Wild West.

A map will not tell you, though, that Alpine's compact population supports no church, no bank, no telephone exchange, no movie house, no parking meter—and only one year-round bar. Nor that the county boasts no doctor, no lawyer, no policeman, no butcher, no barber, no candlestick maker—and the only woman sheriff in California. This is the proper field for conversation.

"Officially," said Mrs. Brown, the only woman sheriff in California, as she checked me into her motel. "Officially, our population here in Markleeville is exactly one hundred. Not much for a county seat, but maybe even that's a shade high. A few of us totaled it up in the bar one night last year and we couldn't go better than fifty-four.

"But Alpine used to be quite a place, you know. The year they created the county—1864 that was—there were eleven thousand people here. But in 1873 the government stopped using silver as legal currency, and inside of two years the population dropped to twelve hundred. Not long afterward Markleeville burned down, so there isn't too much of the old stuff left. What's that? Piute trout? You'd best talk to our Fish and Game man about them. His house is only a step down the road."

The Fish and Game man took just under three minutes to gravitate from trout to population. "Well," he said. "They claim three hundred for the county, but I doubt it. Take Markleeville itself. Nothing like the one hundred it's supposed to have. Let's see, at the motel there's Mrs. Brown and . . ." He began checking off names on his fingers. "Fifty-one," he said at the end of a rapid count. "Yes, fifty-one."

I quoted Mrs. Brown's bar census of fifty-four the previous year.

"That's right—three people left last winter. It's a pretty tight-knit little community, you know; every family has at least one county official—a supervisor or something. These days the place depends pretty much on summer tourists—sportsmen mostly. In winter it's closed up tight. All they keep open is fifteen miles of state road and twelve of county road. To get out to the rest of California you have to go 'round through Nevada. Of course, with everybody thrown so much together it would be expecting too much of human nature for there not to be . . . well, shall we say 'local politics.' On any subject you like to name, the whole county's always divided into at least two warring camps.

"The place had quite a history though. No, I hadn't heard that Chinamen ever logged up Silver King. I guess it's possible, but . . . Tell you what—if you want to find out for sure, stop in at old Harry Hawkins' place. He knows everything that went on, and he's still as sharp as a needle. You'll pass right by his house, the way you're going. It's only four miles out of Markleeville."

"Chinamen?" barked Mr. Hawkins, his well-kept beard shooting out like a lance. "Chinamen logging? Not on your life! Three of 'em ran a placer outfit for a while just beyond Markleeville, but that's the only manual labor I've seen them do anywhere in this county. Mostly they were cooks and the like. No, young fellow, don't you believe a word of it. French Canadians it was, up Silver King. Peak of the logging was in the seventies. Tapered off in the eighties. I remember the last drive myself—in eighty-nine that'd be. Eighty thousand cords went down the river that time.

"Yessir, this county's got quite a history. Came up like a bubble—and burst like one too. All in a hundred years—and I've seen seventy-five of them myself. At one time, two six-horse coaches ran every day up to Silver Mountain City. And as for newspapers, why we had . . ." He strung off a list of names.

"Well, that's six I can think of right off. And look at us today! Population of three hundred—so they say." Mr. Hawkins snorted. "Maybe—if you count in all the Indians and all the Indians' dogs. Yessir, came up like a bubble, and burst like one."

I nodded out of the open front door. "I see from the map that the high point up there is called Hawkins Peak. Was it named after your family?"

"Sure it was. After my grandmother. Came close to being our earliest settler, she did. And she was the one who suggested naming Markleeville after Jacob Marklee. He was a friend of hers and the first man to take up land over there. They found him one morning on his doorstep with his head knocked in, but they never found out who did it."

I asked Mr. Hawkins if he had always lived in the same house.

"Oh no, no. Certainly not. Why, this place is only sixty years old. I was born in a house that used to stand in that patch of willows, two hundred yards down the road. Burnt down long ago though. Mind you, I've managed to make quite a collection in this place. A real House of Mystery it is nowadays. Look . . . taken about 1850, this was. Given to my grandfather back in St. Louis."

I took the photograph. It showed an intense young man with a huge beard hanging down like a swarm of bees. Neatly written across the back was C. C. CARSON.

"They called him Kit," said Mr. Hawkins. "But his real name was Christopher Columbus Carson."

Half an hour later Mr. Hawkins came out to see me off. Before I left, I kneeled down and filled my canteen from a tiny creek that flowed through the garden.

Mr. Hawkins stood looking down at me, smiling. He gave an odd little chuckle that was mostly pride. "That water's been used without a break for one hundred and one years now," he said.

Two mornings later I stood on the crest of the Carson Range.

Back the way I had come, held within its rim of still-white peaks, nestled the "cup" that was Alpine County. I saw now how its lip poured out eastward down the Carson River valley into the Nevada desert. I picked out Hawkins Peak and the hills above Markleeville. And far beyond them I found at last —bright as it always was in morning sunlight—the valley of the Silver King.

I turned around—and looked out over a huge trough. Almost filling it—blue and calm, edges fitting the foothills like glass—spread Lake Tahoe. But I found myself looking beyond the lake to new mountains. For there, among new snowcaps, was the Wild Area.

CHAPTER

9

ALONG THE HIGH SIERRA

The rest of the world quite rightly sees America as a cockpit of rapacity and exploitation. But it tends to forget that America is also a land of altruistic idealism—an idealism that can give birth to magnificently generous concepts, hammer them into tangibilities, and then throw the whole thing open for the rest of humanity to enjoy.

The world is inclined to remember, for example, that early American settlers slashed and gutted the virgin forests of their new continent; that they slaughtered prodigious herds of buffalo almost into extinction; that they did, in other words, what new settlers had always done, everywhere—wage total war against a Nature that to them was the natural enemy. But the world usually ignores the reverse of this coin.

On the night of September 19, 1870, five men sat around a campfire in what was then the territory of Montana. The men were primarily speculators. To confirm rumors of rich mineral and real estate potential, they had penetrated deep into the almost unexplored Yellowstone River wilderness. A month's journeying had shown them commercial potential beyond their wildest dreams; but it had also revealed geysers and canyons, lakes and waterfalls, forests and mountain peaks, and a teeming wildlife. Around the last campfire before they returned to civilization, these five hard-headed businessmen discussed the natural impulse to convert their discoveries into personal profit. But remembering the superb beauty they had seen, they spurned the certainty of wealth. They agreed unanimously that private ownership of the Yellowstone region should never be countenanced, and that "it ought to be set aside by the government and forever held to the unrestricted use of the people."

Back in civilization, they registered no land or minerals claims. Instead, they wrote and lectured on the wonders of Yellowstone's natural beauty. Their words swept across the country. Two years later, President Grant signed into law an act creating the world's first National Park. The revolutionary concept of conserving wilderness for its own sake has now spread to every continent. And in enlightened practice America still leads the way. James Fisher, a visiting English naturalist, recently wrote in his *Wild America*, "Never have I seen such wonders or met landlords so worthy of their land. They had, and still have, the power to ravage it; and instead they have made it a garden."

In Death Valley I had seen an attempt to preserve a part of America essentially as it was when the white man came; but Death Valley has been opened up by roads and amenities, as have most National Parks. In Primitive or Wilderness Areas, all man's travel tools are banned: no roads, no vehicles, no boats. Only hikers and horsemen may use the narrow trails. Compared with some such reservations, the Wild Area in the summit country of the Sierra Nevada above Lake Tahoe is small and almost tame. Its highest peak reaches barely ten thousand feet above sea level. But it is beautiful country. And it is very heavily used.

Lake Tahoe itself—only a four-hour drive for the three million people who live around San Francisco Bay—has become northern California's most popular playground. It has something for everybody. People with money to burn flock like moths to the neon lights of the Nevada shore. There they flutter in ecstasy around the one-armed bandits that have moved in from Reno. People with simpler tastes, shorter pockets, and a yearning for suntans congregate along the California shoreline. They fish, swim, water-ski, and finally barbecue without having to move more than two drinks off the highway. People who prefer the outdoors climb up west of the lake into the Wild Area. And there they find wilderness "set aside by the government and forever held to the unrestricted use of the people."

When I climbed up into the Wild Area I found a new sample of America.

At first, it was lake country. Some of the lakes lay open and crisp and sparkling. Others brooded in retirement, like philosophers. Between the lakes, rough stepping-stones led across creeks that vanished into snowdrifts through blue-gray doorways. Sometimes, bare gray rock was the whole scenery —menacing in shadow, bright and inviting in sunlight. But usually, mile after mile, I walked through forest. And always, high above, towered snow-capped peaks.

After two days I came to the infant Rubicon River and began to follow it northward. And now, sometimes, I found myself on the edge of a meadow with a familiar look—a sunlight-and-shadow, almost-too-good-to-be-true, Silver King kind of a look.

In the week I spent wandering through the fifty miles of Wild Area, I met about half a dozen people a day. And I knew that everyone I met shared one thing with me.

All the way from Mexico, well-intentioned inquirers had been saying, "Oh, but there's an easier way than that! Why don't you take the road to So-and-So?" For them, naturally, country was something that had to be passed through on the way from one place to the next. For me, places were refueling points at the end of a stretch of country. Sometimes I had said, "Don't forget, you're interested in *getting* somewhere; I'm interested in *going*." But the idea did not always get over. Now, up in the Wild Area, I knew that everyone looked at the country with the same eyes as I did.

They had little else in common.

I met men, women, and children. Some rode horses. A few led burros—or tried to. The majority labored along under backpacks: packs that perched high on shoulders and packs that wallowed around buttocks; neat packs like bundles back from the laundry and hippopotamic packs like bundles ready to go there; little pouches as convenient as a kangaroo's and murderous millstones that buckled their bearers' knees. And the people I met were as varied as their burdens—as mixed a bunch as any cross-section of people who happen at a given time to find some common interest attracting them to Union Square, Bond Street, or Fifth Avenue.

To be accurate, I did not always quite "meet" them.

There was the evening that there floated across the Rubicon River the authentic nesting sounds of a troop of Girl Scouts.

There was the early morning, ships-that-pass-in-the-night scene beside a small lake. It was a shady, enclosed place that made me think of Walden Pond. The trail skirted one bank, and I walked slowly, trying to see down into the sunlit water. Suddenly I almost trod on a little blue tackle box. It lay open beside the trail, every compartment overflowing with spinners—red, silver, gold. Set there between two moss-covered tree boles, the box was incongruous yet friendly. I looked around. Except for the box and the narrow trail, there was no sign of man's existence. Then I glimpsed movement. A hundred yards away on the far side of the lake a fisherman stood in deep shadow, a mere silhouette against greenery. I leaned on my staff beside the tackle box, watching him. After a while he looked up. I waved. He waved back. Then I went on down the trail, and within twenty paces the lake was hidden and I was back in thick forest.

Often, though, I stopped and talked to those I met.

There was the elderly man who might have been a judge and whose voice and thoughts were quiet and contemplative but who sat his horse like Thor taking a weekend off from making thunder.

There were the father and eleven-year-old son, engrossed in a private world, their two fly-decked caps close together as they debated which streamer was most likely to tempt the trout of Lake Aloha. We discussed this problem, and even weightier ones.

Afterward, as I climbed up beyond the lake, father and son were fishing side by side at the foot of a snow-terraced rock face. They looked very much alone, very much together. Not many youngsters are so lucky, I thought. Not many fathers either.

Then there was the day I climbed a peak on the edge of the Wild Area, overlooking Lake Tahoe. For three hours the panorama had opened out below me with that slow, unfolding growth—inevitable, but full of surprises—that is one of the rewards of climbing a mountain. About noon, almost at the peak, I crossed a rocky spur. And there, four thousand feet below, I saw the whole huge basin of Lake Tahoe.

I heard myself gasp and say out loud, "My God, what a color!"

I walked up to the peak, sat down beside the metal summit marker, and gave myself up to the blue-and-greenness of forest and lake and sky. The air was all light and space and silence. I leaned back against warm rock. The sun beat down, timelessly.

After a while a scraping sound, as of a fair-sized animal, came from just beyond the summit marker. I fixed my eyes on a ledge, less than six feet away. I had noticed that beyond it the rock sloped away quite gently. I waited, every muscle still. And then, up over the ledge, outlined against blue sky, looking straight into my eyes, appeared a boy's head. It stopped dead. It was cheerful, out of breath, and as surprised as I was. It looked very young to be at almost ten thousand feet on its own, even attached to a body.

I felt I ought to say something. "Did you come all the way up by yourself?" I asked.

"Oh no, Mommy's just behind." The boy climbed up onto the ledge. "Yes, there she is." And a little way below us appeared a tall, slim woman in shorts and a red windbreaker. She waved at her son, then stopped. "Ah, the Old Man of the Mountains!" she called out cheerfully.

She walked on up toward us. Her walk was the rare kind that goes equally well with shorts on a mountain and with an evening dress in a ballroom. As she came up close she said, "Oh no, the *Young* Man of the Mountains!" and I felt better.

She had thick, dark hair, and it was difficult to believe that the eleven- or twelve-year-old boy was her son.

"Isn't it a fantastic view?" she said. "Peter and I often come up. Nowadays, as you see, he gets here first." She sat down, and we discussed climbing mountains and walking from Mexico to Oregon. Her name was Jinny. I found some snow on a sheltered terrace, lit my pressure stove, and brewed tea for the three of us. Jinny provided sandwiches. Afterward I apologized for having no cigarettes to offer.

Jinny smiled. "Oh, I never seem to want to smoke out of doors anyway. I guess . . . I guess I don't really enjoy smoking much. In itself, I mean. At a party now, it's different. A cigarette takes away the taste of the liquor—and without one I'd never know what to do with my hands." She smiled again. "It's wonderful how honest a mountain makes you, isn't it?"

She got up and walked forward and stood looking out over the blueness of Lake Tahoe. Suddenly she stretched her whole body ecstatically. "Oh what a wonderful world it is!" she said. "Three weeks ago my husband and I were in Hawaii, skin-diving and climbing mountains. And now dear old Tahoe again. You know, I feel sorry for people who never discover this kind of thing. The day we left Hawaii, some friends of ours flew in. The moment they got inside the hotel they rushed for a bridge table, and we knew they'd spend their whole vacation playing bridge and drinking. What a waste! I'm afraid we Americans sometimes forget how lucky we are."

I met "Twig" just outside the Wild Area; but he was essentially a part of it. When he bounced up in his jeep, I was changing film beside an old stagecoach road that is one of the Area's boundaries. We sat and talked, looking back up the rock-bound Rubicon Valley.

"Yes, I backpack in whenever I can," said Twig. "But somehow there's not often time these days. That's why I bought this jeep. But walking's the way to travel all right. Ever since Henry Ford, we Americans have been getting soft. I can still remember my great-grandmother, and she'd crossed the United States seven times. And every time except one, when there happened to be an empty wagon, she walked."

Twig nodded up the valley, carrying the gesture far beyond the horizon. "All the way from Mexico, huh?" He sighed. "When I left school, my mother talked me into taking a degree and going into engineering. But I often wish I'd stayed a backwoods cowpuncher and taken pack trains in, like I did when I was a kid. Still, it's good to know that when the pressures build up you can get away from it all and come out to places like this."

It was then, I think, that I realized what was obvious enough really: that the Wild Area was not only a new sample of America; it was a microcosm of The Walk. It was a place where people could do for a few snatched hours or days what I was lucky enough to be doing for six months.

The realization made me more aware of all the small events that sometimes passed unnoticed because they had become part of the fabric of my life: the first clouds of the day forming over distant peaks; a scarlet snow plant sticking up through the carpet of dead leaves and looking at once succulent as strawberries and deadly as a toadstool; a very small trout following an enormous low-flying bumblebee to the river's edge and turning back at the last moment with a flounce of its tail; a turquoise-breasted hummingbird hovering ten inches from my nose and inspecting my red shirt for pollen; a lizard sunbathing on rough granite and looking me over with the critical eye of a mother-in-law elect.

There was one such moment when everything the Wild Area offered—everything The Walk stood for—came together. For three days I had been following the Rubicon River as it grew by slow degrees from brawling infancy into staid maturity. I had just waded across it and was sitting on a grassy bank, putting my boots back on. The cold river had been refreshing, and now the sun was warm. A copper-red dragonfly landed deftly on a blade of grass at the water's edge, so close I could have touched it.

And suddenly thankfulness surged through me. Thankfulness for the moment, for the day, for the freedom of The Walk, for life itself.

I sat quite still, one boot half on, holding my breath and willing memory to imprison that instant of time—to capture and hold every particle of it. I wanted the copper-red dragonfly on its blade of green grass, curving out over the blue Rubicon. I wanted the warm sunshine and the rough grassy bank. I wanted the scent of lupines and the sound of running water. I wanted the deep forest shadow on the far bank. I wanted the snowbanks that hung high above it. I even wanted the mosquitoes on my bare arms. I knew that later I would find it difficult to believe I had really wanted the mosquitoes; but at that moment I was glad for their sakes that they were alive, and I wanted them too.

The moment did not last long. The dragonfly's wings trembled; it flew away. The blade of grass straightened. I finished putting on my boots, heaved the pack onto my back, and started once more down the trail.

Before long the sun dropped behind a line of stark peaks. Down on the valley floor it was suddenly very gray. But I knew that the copper-red dragonfly beside the Rubicon had given me something I would never altogether lose. And I knew that it was for moments like these that people came to the Wild Area.

Wilderness would be worth conserving if it did nothing but make such moments possible. And as I walked I found myself wishing I could thank the five men who had sat around their Yellowstone campfire in the fall of 1870. It would have been satisfying for them to know that their altruism that night—their altruism in a cockpit of rapacity and exploitation—had done so much not only for me but for the nesting Girl Scouts and for Thor astride his horse and for the father and son fishing in Lake Aloha and for Jinny stretching ecstatically on the mountaintop and for Twig in his jeep and for millions of other Americans and for millions more, born and yet to be born, all over the world.

One evening I came down into a steep-sided little valley and found an abandoned ranch house, tucked away and forgotten. As I walked into the homestead, a herd of cattle stampeded away in panic, kicking up clouds of fine dust. The dust hung long afterward among the trees, making the place look as if it had been bombed. I lit my stove on the steps of a crumbling stone hayloft. Dusk fell. Three deer wandered past—vague brown shadows against a background of dying bracken and hanging brown dust. I walked across the farmyard and found a rusty faucet. Close by, a coyote yowled. The sound echoed up the valley.

As I filled my canteen at the faucet, I kept looking at a sage-covered bank. It was some minutes before I understood why I was doing so. Sagebrush is a sign of heat and dryness, of desert or semi-desert; and this sage was the first I had seen since I climbed up into the High Sierra. And all at once I realized that the ridges above me were lower than those I had become used to. The soil was dustier, the trees so much thinner that you almost had to call them spindly.

The mountains were tapering off.

I went back to the old hayloft, sat down beside my stove, and studied the map. The confused highland mass that lay ahead could be called a side branch of the Sierra Nevada, but its elevation was much less than I had realized. It would almost certainly be drier than what I had come to think of as

Sierra country. And the foothills soon sank away. Within two days I would be out in semi-desert.

Next day I found once more, as I had done when I came near to the end of the desert, that the surest way of savoring something to the full is to become aware that it is almost over.

I climbed an escarpment on the far side of the valley and came back into thick forest. And now I kept noticing, as if they were something new, little things that had become so much a part of my life since I climbed up out of the desert that I had come to take them for granted. The ground sloped gently downward, and soon there were little clearings, thick with skunk cabbage. A rivulet threaded through tall grass. Every ripple and every blade formed a part of the pattern of texture, part of the pattern of light and shade. A crimson columbine curtsied to a turquoise dragonfly. A thin brown snake, basking away its afternoon on a stone, slid off at my approach and swam down into the darkness of a pool. And always, consciously now, I was walking among trees.

All day, as I walked, I found myself listening. In the desert, the cicadas rasp and there is no doubt about it; but in the forest there is sometimes, you think, a buzzing, almost a rasping among the trees. It is a soothing and yet intriguing sound that comes from nowhere and everywhere. Sometimes it is the distorted echo of running water. Sometimes it is the wind in the treetops. And sometimes it is nothing you can name. That day I could not name it, but I heard it more clearly than ever.

All day the ground sloped away. The forest thinned. The trees grew thinner too, became undeniably spindly. The rivulet joined Sagehen Creek, and there was sagebrush again. At first it grew in isolated clumps. Then in large patches. By afternoon it stretched away, acre after acre, as far as I could see down the valley.

Late in the evening, I was almost ready to camp when I saw a man coming toward me on a parallel trail, a few feet to one side. The semi-darkness failed to hide a certain oddness about him, but I could not decide if it lay in his clothes or in his walk or in something else.

I half checked my stride, wanting to talk but not knowing quite how to begin. "Evening," I said.

"Evening," the man answered. He hesitated too, and the black-and-white collie at his heels almost ran into him. Then he resumed his slow, easy stride and vanished into the dusk.

I was still wondering about him when I camped on a dusty sagebrush flat.

While dinner cooked, I did some calculating. I knew that now the mountains were almost over, The Walk would move into a new stage. It was still two hundred miles to the Oregon border, even in a straight line. Walking, it would probably be half as far again. For various reasons—some of them quite sensible—I wanted to be at the boundary by the end of the first week in September. That left me just over three weeks. To make the border on schedule, I would on most traveling days have to walk a good twenty miles.

Before I went to sleep I made up my mind that, no matter what distractions tempted me, the next day would be the first of the twenty-milers. And the most important thing was to get moving as early as possible.

I woke at dawn to the sound of bells. A large flock

of sheep was browsing slowly toward me. In the center of the dust storm they created, rising up out of it like an iceberg from fog, moved a brown burro with a bell around its neck. By the time I had finished a hurried breakfast, sheep and dust surrounded me.

I had just strapped the sleeping bag onto my pack when a man appeared on the edge of the flock. I recognized him at once. The black-and-white collie still followed at his heels.

"Morning," said the man.

"Morning," I answered.

The man pushed slowly toward me through the sheep. There was indeed something old-fashioned and quaint about his much-worn tweed suit. And something old-fashioned and dignified about the way he moved and about the way he smiled, taking his time over it, as he reached me.

"I hope my sheep have not caused you inconvenience," he said. He spoke with a European accent.

"Not in the least," I said. "I was glad they woke me up."

"Good," said the man. "Very glad." He took tobacco and cigarette papers from a side pocket of his coat.

And suddenly I realized that he must be one of the Basque sheepherders I had been hoping to meet ever since I saw the blackened names on the aspens beside Silver King Creek.

We chatted about the country ahead. The Basque had herded in the Warner Mountains, up near the Oregon border, during World War I. As he talked about it, he rolled a cigarette, coaxing the tobacco into shape with the care of a potter working clay.

Once or twice he smiled his slow-emerging smile. It gave him an unexpected kind of Maurice Chevalier charm.

I was settling down for a long discussion when I brought myself up short. As soon as I could do it without rudencss, I tried to explain why I had to push on. Somehow it didn't sound very convincing.

But the Basque smiled understandingly. "You are right," he said, giving his cigarette a final pat. "To start early is the only way."

I pushed through to the edge of the flock. The Basque still stood where I had left him, knee-deep in sheep and the pall of dust. I waved my staff. He waved back.

Then I turned and went down the valley. As I walked, sagebrush scratched at my legs.

CHAPTER

10

DOWN THE HOME STRETCH

Two days later I came to the edge of some trees and found myself looking out over a new and unexpected openness. Northward as far as I could see stretched a broad, dry valley. It was treeless and sage-covered. On either side, hills rose naked and smooth.

When I walked down into the valley, the sense of openness came with me. It was not the spaciousness you feel on a mountaintop; nothing is open quite like that. It was more like the sweep of an empty beach. And all at once I recognized the old familiar openness of the desert.

Soon there were more desert echoes. I crossed a Western Pacific track and heard, exactly as I had heard at Goffs beside the Atchison, Topeka and Santa Fe, a tenuous Hindu chant that by degrees gained definition and rhythm and volume until it erupted into a pounding climax of percussion. I turned north along a highway. Cars bore down from the tapering distance, flashed past, and left the dusty aftertaste I remembered from months before in the part-tamed desert beside the Colorado. And when rain clouds rolled up from the south and a light rain began, it brought a clean and familiar fragrance. The clouds grew blacker, the rain heavier. The rain bounced back like sword points from the shining highway, stinging my legs. The wind drove me forward and wrapped the poncho around me, and I found myself flinging out songs for it to snatch away as it had done in the storm beyond Earp.

And yet, after the rain had stopped and sunshine had first created a new freshness and then burned it away, the desert was not as I remembered it. There were no flowers, and that had something to do with the difference. But something else was missing from the dead sameness of sagebrush that stretched out on either side of the straight black road. At first I could not decide what it was.

It took me four days to find out.

I was skirting east of Honey Lake, away from the highway, through monotonous sagebrush. In late afternoon I came to a huddle of buildings that had once been Amadee Hot Springs Hotel. (Somebody had told me that a boat used to serve it across Honey Lake; but the lake had dried up for a time, and the hulk of the boat was still lying somewhere along the shoreline.) Near the buildings, gray clouds belched out from an assortment of orifices and drifted across the sagebrush. A few soiled chickens kept crystallizing from the edges of the steam, then dissolving again.

Beside the buildings stood a tractor and some farm implements. As I approached, a man came down the dirt road, leading two draft horses. He was round-shouldered and droop-mouthed, bludgeoned into perpetual boredom.

"It looks pretty dry here for farming," I said. "Do you have to haul your drinking water in?"

The man jerked his head at the nearest belch of steam. "Cool that stuff," he said, and spat.

All afternoon, dark clouds had been building up. Now, a few drops of rain fell. "Does it usually rain much here, this time of year?" I said.

"Been lots o' rain this fall," said the man.

I felt a momentary shock. It was the first time anyone had suggested that summer was over.

Almost at once, I recognized that what I had missed in the desert ever since I came down from the mountains was the bustle and energy of spring.

And afterward, as I walked on through the desolate sagebrush, I realized with an even greater shock that, like summer, The Walk was nearly over. I had known all along, of course, that it would end in early September. In a sense, I had known it when I took the first step northward from the Mexican border. But this was the first time I had looked at the end as something that was really going to happen. And now here it was, suddenly and disconcertingly, as close and probable as next payday.

Partly because of the monotonous country, partly because of the need to hurry, I walked for most of the final two hundred miles along roads—first a highway, then farm and fire roads. The days were drawing in fast, but with easy going underfoot I made my regular twenty miles a day comfortably enough.

As I walked, I kept thinking back to the early

weeks along the Colorado. Then, soft feet and layers of city fat had meant that in any one day I could walk, at most, ten or fifteen miles. And I had had to take frequent rest days. Now, although my feet still needed taking care of, they certainly did not limit mileage. That stage was long past. And I was twenty pounds lighter. "Fit like a bear" as one man had put it.

But walking had never become effortless. People often said, "I guess you're so used to the pack by now that it doesn't worry you." But only on those rare occasions that the load fell below forty pounds could I sometimes forget it. At fifty pounds I could not. At sixty the pack was heavy. And at seventy it took the joy out of walking. Short side trips with no load on my back were still like running into the sea after a hot day in the city.

But the pack had long ago become something I felt affection for, something that meant home and comfort. And when, looking ahead, I began to think of my apartment, I found it hard to readjust to the idea that before long "home" would once again be a place of curtains and carpets and a refrigerator instead of the five square yards of California over which I happened at each halt to spread "the house on my back."

Now, whenever I camped, "home" looked much the same. I sat on my faded green sleeping bag and leaned back between the pockets of the pack. The pack was propped up against the walking staff or a tree. My feet, bare or moccasined, stuck out in front of me, down at the far end of the "house." At night, my boots became the "office." They stood close beside my head, crammed full of maps, pen, notebook, spectacles, and other pocket furniture.

Six inches beyond the "office," the "kitchen" began. It centered on the little pressure stove I had bought for use above timberline on White Mountain and had found so convenient that I used it all the rest of the way. If it was lunchtime, water was heating on the stove in the larger of my two nesting cook pots, with the smaller pot perched on top, being "hotted" in Britannic tradition for the tea that half of the water would make. Beside the stove stood the stainless steel Sierra Club cup. Food for the current meal, each item in its own plastic bag, completed the "kitchen."

The rest of the food was pushed out of the way on the other side of the sleeping bag, up by the pack. Beside it went other things I had taken out of the pack but was not using—the current paperback book perhaps, the aluminum stove cover (doubling as spare cup, but murderously hot on lips), and the frying pan I carried in trout country. My hat hung, with cameras and binoculars, on the pack frame. Everything went into its place with no more thought than I would give to putting back my apartment furniture after a party.

And practice had sandpapered most other domestic detail into a fine art. Or, rather, into automatic action. I have never been one of those people who spring to life each morning the moment their eyes open. But now I could get through the painful reawakening process with as little thought as getting out of bed at home and stumbling in a daze to the shower. Waking time was governed partly by the time I went to sleep, mostly by conscious effort. In desert or semi-desert I usually managed to wake at first light. In the mountains, where ground frost or dew meant drying everything out in the sun and where cooler days made an early start unnecessary, I woke about sunrise. Whatever the time, I dedicated several minutes to sloth. Then I put on shirt and sweater (in cold weather I had been sleeping on the sweater) and sat up and leaned back against the pack. I reached out behind me, pulled my shorts from their place just under the pack flap, and from the ticket pocket took a book of matches. I pushed the shorts down into the sleeping bag to warm (the matches stayed overnight in the shorts so that I would do the warming business automatically) then lit the pressure stove and put on the larger pot, filled with water the night before. Within five minutes, tea was ready. By then I had begun to munch the dehydrated fruit that had been soaking overnight in the second pot. Sometimes I added milk, cereal, or chocolate to the fruit. After breakfast, if there was any water at all, I washed my feet. If there was plenty of water, I washed the pans. Afterward—still in my sleeping bag if it was cold—I stowed everything away in the pack. Then I got up quickly, hoisted the pack onto my back, and starting walking. Within half an hour I was awake.

All day, "household affairs" sorted themselves out without waste of time. Deciding how much water to carry no longer meant a drawn-out balancing of weight against safety. I knew that in temperatures touching ninety, one gallon would last me thirty miles with no appreciable discomfort—but with no washing or tooth cleaning either. Half a gallon was a comfortable ration for eating, tooth cleaning, and rudimentary washing at a dry night stop—provided I was sure of finding more by mid-morning. Ever since the last leg of southern desert I had, when water posed any problem at all, tended to make dry night stops. During the heat of the day I rested up at water. In the cool of evening I walked for an hour or two, camped wherever nightfall found me, and moved on to water next morning. This way I rarely carried more than half a gallon; and during my midday rest I had unlimited water for washing pots and pans, clothes, and myself. Sometimes I had a swimming pool too. At night, the campsite rarely mattered much, but when it did I weighed up almost automatically such factors as water, firewood, shade, wind (always *down* desert canyons at night), and exact directions of sunrise (important for early morning comfort in cold weather, and easily checked by compass). I no longer gave much conscious thought to building a cooking fire (double-V-stick-with-crossbar whenever possible) or to siting it in relation to the big fire I often built for cheer and warmth. At one dry night camp, with no water to spare for washing, I happened to notice that exactly forty minutes after halting, without hurrying in any way, I had cooked and eaten supper and was in bed already half asleep.

When I stopped to consider, I was surprised to find how automatically I did a hundred little domestic chores that experience had taught me were worthwhile: stuffing empty plastic food bags into the pack frame at halts so that they would not blow away; filling the pressure stove with white gas immediately after lunch so that it would not run dry in the dark (one fill each day almost always saw me through); putting dehydrated potatoes and a cupful of water in the inner cooking pot an hour or so before night camp so that they would soak soft while I walked and would cook in five or ten minutes instead of half an hour.

But I was still learning. To save space in the pack, I had almost from the beginning strapped my sleeping bag outside it. For several days on the last leg, the threat of rain made me cram the bag inside. I was surprised at how much better this balanced the load. Again, I had never found a wholly satisfactory container for such small items as salt tablets, medical supplies, and fishing lures. Plastic vials tended to crack; anything else was too heavy or too fragile. It was only in the final week that I thought of aluminum 35-mm film containers.

As I walked on northward along the highway, I found myself comparing these domestic details with their civilized equivalents: buying groceries, taking a shower, lighting the stove. On The Walk, such chores played a bigger part than at home. But they contributed much more. And now, because the end was near, I found myself suddenly aware of them; aware of—and strangely comforted by—sounds and sensations that had become the unnoticed constants of my life. I found myself listening to the scrape of the metal spoon against the metal pot lid that doubled as a plate. I heard the rhythm of my boots and staff, and remembered their different inflections on sand and on soil and on rock. I noticed once more the quiet rub of binoculars against the aluminum pack frame, and the slight but incessant rattle of the camera filter in its plastic case, deep in my pants pocket. I listened for the familiar creak of leather harness as it settled back in place after a halt—then discovered that I was enjoying the self-reliant feeling of the pack's weight, heavy on my shoulders. And in the evening I found myself looking forward with new pleasure to the moment when I would pull on the tapes of my mummy bag and shut myself off in a private world with the stars.

Such nostalgia was not, I suppose, really surprising. For after five months and a thousand miles, these simple things had become as much a part of The Walk as deer tracks in the dust or the champagne taste of mountain water.

There is a difference in shape between a journey as it happens and a journey as you remember it. At the time, there it is—day after roughly equal day. But when you look back afterward (and especially when you talk or write about it) memory pushes and pulls at time as if it were a concertina. The vivid moments expand, so that they stand out like cameos. The dull periods contract, until whole weeks become compressed into thin shims.

The final three weeks of The Walk were, by and large, dull. I walked mostly along roads that held me at arm's length from the countryside. For the first time since Mexico, the country was, in any case, too monotonous to keep my mind fully occupied. And I was hurrying now in a steady and determined way that I had not done before, even in Death Valley.

On top of all this, and perhaps even more important, there was the sense of ending. Once I had realized that The Walk was almost over, my mind refused to stay chained to the present. It kept jumping ahead to plan the future—the future beyond the Oregon border—then wandering back through the days and weeks and months of desert and mountains.

It was, I suppose, a blend of these two things—the dullness of the country and the sense of ending—that turned the final leg into a disjointed affair, into something quite different from what had gone before. By the time I reached the Oregon boundary, the final three weeks of the journey had already contracted in my memory, so that little remained except isolated cameos.

Some of the cameos fixed themselves in my memory because the country, dull as it was, still produced "firsts."

For months now, the yowl of coyotes had been almost as common a background to the days and nights as the rattle of cable cars had been in my San Francisco apartment. And then, early one morning, I saw a coyote trotting across an open space in the sagebrush. At least, I assumed it was a coyote. I was surprised to discover that I did not know quite what a coyote looked like, other than being doggy.

A day or two later, I stood and watched a porcupine flubbel away into the trees like a bristling jelly bag. And when I stopped to think about it, I found that I could not remember having seen a porcupine before.

Some scenes seemed to lodge in my memory for no apparent reason—or at least for no reason that was apparent at the time.

The sun rose, and I struck camp and walked toward an embankment of the Western Pacific Railroad that separated me from the highway. A train was approaching. I waited. The locomotive thundered closer, shining and beautiful. The huge eye in its forehead acknowledged me with a feeble but friendly greeting. I waved. An arm waved back from the cab. Then the massive wheels were above me, all modern power and arrogance. Then the Pullmans were pounding past, dragging the air along and shaking the sand beneath my feet. And then the taillight was winking red, and I was once more alone in the quiet desert.

Beyond the village of Ravendale I left the highway and followed dirt roads into the foothills of the Warner Mountains. Scattered juniper trees began to leaven the monotony of the sagebrush, and soon they gave way to pines and a few tentative aspen groves. As I walked into one of the aspen groves, looking for a campsite, the light was already failing; but I could make out names and dates carved into the silvery bark of several trees. The carvings were black with age, as they had been beside the Silver King, and I felt once again that time had in some way dignified them and justified a practice that normally disgusts me. Most of the names were unreadable; but one stood out clearly: ENRIKE SEPTUAIN. I remembered my Basque sheepherder as I had last seen him, knee deep in sheep and a pall of dust, waving good-bye. He had herded up here in the Warner Mountains during World War I. And as I stood in front of the aspen tree, looking at the blackened carving, I found myself wondering, hopefully, if his name could possibly have been Enrike Septuain.

Sometimes, it was obvious enough why a cameo stuck in my memory.

To restock and refuel, I came down onto the plain again, into Alturas. The evening I left Alturas and headed back toward the Warner Mountains, I walked briefly beside the highway. And as I walked a certain car came toward me, moving quite slowly. A man and a woman sat in front. They were neither entwined like adolescents nor segregated like married strangers. They sat upright and adult, linked by an indefinable, satisfied companionship.

For six months I had not ridden in a car. I had almost forgotten what it felt like. And I had not been sorry. But now I turned and watched this car dwindle into the distance. And I waited until it had disappeared before I turned and walked on toward the mountains.

Certain events carry a delayed action significance. A scene may seem unimportant in itself; but you detect an unexpected incisiveness about it, a momentary knife-edge. You sense something meaningful in the tilt of a girl's head or in the angle at which a bar of sunlight strikes a doorway. Deep inside you, a mechanism registers. "Something is happening," it says. "I cannot tell you just what it is or what it means; but remember this moment." Without knowing, you remember. Later, sometimes months later, the scene snaps with a click into its place in life's jigsaw. You remember the scene as vividly as if you held a photograph in your hand. More vividly: you know not only how the light slanted but how the wind felt or a man's voice sounded. And through all the erosions of time you never quite forget what you saw. It persists, like those trivial incidents of childhood that live on unexpectedly down the years. And occasionally you recall with surprise how, at the time, you felt acid etching the picture on your memory.

I had walked barely a mile along the road that led up into the Warner Mountains when the car snapped with a click into its jigsaw. I saw again the man and the woman sitting side by side.

And suddenly I wanted the comforts of everyday life. I wanted the key to my apartment. I wanted regular hot showers. I wanted my car again. I even remembered with nostalgia the eternal hunt for parking space. For more than a thousand miles I had traveled alone and it had never occurred to me to feel lonely; but now, above all, I wanted companionship. I was ready at last for The Walk to end.

On the last lap of all I walked along the spine of the Warner Mountains. Eastward rolled the Nevada desert. Westward, beyond a hundred miles of lava beds, the white-tipped wraith that was Mount Shasta became at sunset a black cone against blood-red sky. One night I camped beside a creek, on a sandy bank that was carpeted with red and brown leaves. Sometime during the night I came half awake. Moonlight was streaming down through a gap in the trees. It centered on my little camp like a pale blue spotlight. All around me, the red and brown leaves were colorless now, but still sad and autumnal. Beyond the spotlight, the forest was black. I do not think I saw anything else, except silhouetted treetops, far overhead. But before I drifted back to sleep I felt a deep sense of ending. It was half sad and half expectant.

Two mornings later I was walking along a dirt road when a yellow, smoke-billowing truck pounded past. Its load of timber was scarred and ugly; but for once the anger that logging stirs up in me was swamped by something else. Yellow logging trucks pounding along between dark trees were something my memory connected with the word "Oregon."

I hurried on northward. A little before noon I cut

away from the road toward the boundary between California and Oregon. The map showed that it was also a national forest boundary. I climbed a slope, threading my way through thin trees. Now that the end was close, I found that I was feeling nothing at all. I crossed an open space with a grove of aspens in its center. Then there was a wire fence, and on it a sign that said NATIONAL FOREST BOUNDARY. I walked up to the fence and put one foot under its lowest strand, onto the ground beyond.

The Walk was over.

It was six months to the hour since I had taken my first step northward from the Mexican border.

And all at once the numbness had gone and I was feeling again. I found myself shouting "Yoho!" and then, once more, "Yoho! Yoho!" The sound lingered among the trees. And behind its foolishness I heard the whoop of victory.

I photographed myself at the fence, then sat down beside it and lit my little stove and put on water for soup and tea.

Inevitably, now that I had reached its physical end, I found myself looking back at The Walk and trying to explain why it had so obviously been a success. But, as had happened before the start, I found when I looked for "reasons" that I was at something of a loss.

There was no doubt, of course, about my having "discovered America." I had been to its lowest point and to within 250 feet of its highest. I had traveled well over half the distance between its southern and northern borders. I had seen its space and its wildness. I had seen a new side of the paradoxes inherent in its sprawl and seeth: carefully conserved wilderness, the envy of every civilized country; crass billboards, making the fast buck at any price; appalling roadside litter that turned whole strips of desert and forest into slums; hospitality that does not come any warmer, anywhere. And I had seen an America that was passing. For by "America" I had meant, all along, the unbelievably varied sample that is California. And, every day, more than a thousand people were moving into the state to live. Tomorrow's California would not, sadly, be the same as today's. And that made The Walk something that could never quite be repeated.

Then there had been the people.

Before I moved to the United States, the editor of a well-known magazine had written me: "I am afraid you will find that there is no such thing as 'a voice of authority' in this country; every man has to extract the truth as best he can from a babel of many voices. The best of luck . . . in the United States; I hope you will find it satisfying, and I'm reasonably sure that you won't find it dull."

I had heard many voices all right. Ira and Corinne asking me to find them "a new frontier." The roadside picnicker—compact, virile, rising forty—who left her companions and came running after me to ask breathlessly, "Do you know anything about spacecraft?" The manager of a Colorado fishing camp who said wistfully, "You're doing just the kind of thing I've often thought about. I've always wanted to get snowed in all winter in a cabin full of books—like in a book I read once. But what with the wife and kids I guess I'll never get the chance now." The man with a vaguely familiar bulldog face who stuck out his hand and said, "British, eh? Well, shake hands with Winston Churchill's third cousin." The Darby-and-Joan couple who entertained me in the garden of their rose-covered cottage and fed me on caramel cake and wild plums. A ranch-hand in a roadside cafe who, hearing of yet another accident just up the way, gave it as his considered opinion that "there ought to be country roads and cow trails and that's all. These highways ain't safe to use no more." The highway construction supervisor who nodded through a cafe window up at White Mountain and said in his slow Louisiana drawl, "Some of these tourists who pull in for a cup of coffee keep staring up there and say, 'Just *look* at that goddam mountain! What a thing to have hanging over you all the while!' Then they go out and get into their cars and rush on again—and I just feel sorry for them."

Yes, I had heard babel all right. It had certainly been satisfying. And anything but dull. Perhaps, given time, I might be able to extract from it some grains of truth about the sprawling restlessness that is America.

But I had known all along that discovering America was only a defensive "reason," only a hook on which to hang something even more worthwhile. I had thought that at the end I would see the real reasons clearly. But it had not happened that way.

I sometimes seemed to be coming close to a valid answer when I remembered ill-defined thoughts that floated through my mind as I squatted in front of a campfire, gazing into its pulsating caverns—"dreaming the fire," as they say in Swahili. Living the way I was, I existed, very consciously, as an atom among the forces of nature, among the huge forces that shape the earth's crust, that regulate the ebb and flow of seasons, that weave and hold in balance all the delicate and interlocking strands that constitute the web of life—the flowers and the rattlesnakes and the coyotes and the men. And as I squatted and "dreamed the fire" I would feel a truth that we usually have to stop and tell ourselves intellectually. I would accept, in a new and fuller sense, that we are, in everything we do, an integral part of this planet's complexity. And such acceptance is something you can all too quickly lose when you live, always, in a city.

But the fact was that I did not really need "reasons." The Walk had been a sprawling and untidy thing, not a neat little package you could label and stack away. I needed to remember only one thing about it: it had worked.

Seven months earlier, the idea of walking up California had burst on me at three o'clock in the morning as I lay awake worrying about the things we all worry about. The problems had crowded so thick that they threatened to overwhelm me: I had wanted, desperately, to "get away from it all." But now I wanted to "get back to it all." I think I had been half afraid of this moment of ending. Afraid of the letdown and emptiness that can come at the end of something that has filled the horizons of your life. Afraid of the loss of purpose, even of identity, that can overwhelm you at the end of a war or a book or a marriage. But now that the moment had come, I found I was eager to grapple once more with the complexities that are the essence of modern life. I could even, with new perspectives to guide me, glimpse something of what cities are all about. And now that The Walk was over, it was quite unthinkable that I should have failed to accept the idea that burst in on me so unexpectedly, seven months before. Now, at the end, I could see that

The Walk had turned out to be its own justification. And that was enough.

I knew, of course, that time would blunt my new sense of purpose. But that did not matter too much. Now, when I needed renewal, I knew where to look.

The water boiled. I turned off the stove for the last time. I noticed with surprise, as I always did, how quiet everything was afterward.

When I had finished the soup and tea, there was only one more thing to be done. I put everything away in the pack, trying not to feel false emotion at such a simple act. Then I walked back down the hill for a hundred yards to the aspen grove in the open space. And for the first time in my life—remembering the Basque sheepherders and feeling that for me too it was justified, just this once—I carved my name on a tree. I carved it in full. And underneath I put:

CALIFORNIA
1958

MEXICO MAR 8
OREGON SEP 8

Then I walked down through the trees toward the road that would take me back to San Francisco and everything the city now offered.

About the Author

Colin Fletcher has never settled down for very long to a prosaic, workaday life. And he seems to operate on the naive assumption that if a man wants something badly enough he can always get it. Yet he has consistently avoided disaster by a healthy margin.

Born in Wales and educated in England, he served during World War II as a captain in the Royal Marine Commandos. In 1947 he emigrated to Africa. After a brief spell as hotel manager ("Not my line," he says), he farmed for four years in Kenya and found the life interesting and satisfying. But it lacked stimulation. He determined to see the world—and to write.

He drove to Southern Rhodesia where, rather to his surprise, he built a road over a virgin mountain. He reconnoitered the terrain on horseback, laid out the alignment with instruments, drove the only bulldozer on the job, and supervised the ditching gang.

After six months back in Britain he set out for the New World. He crossed the Atlantic by tending a planeload of cattle from Ireland to New York, hitchhiked to Toronto, then drove a new car on delivery to the West. His fare from London to Vancouver, B.C., totaled ten dollars. For three summers he prospected and laid out roads in northern and western Canada.

In 1956 he moved to California, where he still lives. Five years after his thousand-mile summer, he made the first known foot-traverse the length of the Grand Canyon, and *The Man Who Walked Through Time* (available from Vintage) describes that journey. Since then, Fletcher has written his best-selling *Complete Walker*, *New Complete Walker*, and *Complete Walker III*, *The Winds of Mara*, and *The Man From the Cave*.

NATURE/OUTDOORS

A minor classic, this is the spellbinding account of a journey on foot from one end of California to the other—from Mexico to Oregon—that the author of *The Complete Walker* and *The Man Who Walked Through Time* took in 1958, two ye[illegible]r he had moved to the United States.

The idea [illegible] him one sleepless night in his San Francisco ap[illegible] without his knowing why. But when people began [illegible]im about it, he replied that he wanted "to tak[illegible] at America." He could scarcely have chosen a [illegible]ied sample.

His route too[illegible]0 miles up the Colorado River, across the Mojav[illegible], through the trough of Death Valley, over 14,24[illegible]igh White Mountain and through the High [illegible] He discovered an unspoiled ghost town, visited [illegible]ontiers, and met an extraordinary variety of people. At the end he had not only discovered America, he had gained a new perspective on his life—and all human lives.

Today, as he notes in the Preface, "Time has given this book a dimension I did not plan.... I did not know that man would soon lay a heavy, engineering hand on much of the land I was seeing.... And now those who know today's California—today's America, today's world—may perhaps find in the book a quiet testimony not only to the past but also, I hope, to the road we must walk in the future."

ISBN 0-394-74631-7